The Best
Is
Yet To Be

Harlan K. Temple

"The Best Is Yet To Be"

Scriptures taken from the Holy Bible, New International Version (NIV)

Cover design by: Prairie Hearth Publishing, LLC
Editor: Loretta Sorensen, Prairie Hearth Publishing, LLC
2310 Willowdale Rd, Yankton, SD 57078

Paperback ISBN: 978-1-7923-7844-7

Available wherever books are sold

prairie hearth
publishing, llc

DEDICATION

I dedicate this book to my beloved wife, Rita;
to my parents, Arleigh and Sophie;
and to my sisters, Ardie and Joanie.
Their love and support has and continues
to be an invaluable element of my life.

FOREWORD

The story of Harlan Temple's life is an inspiring testimony to what can be accomplished and how full and fulfilling a life can be in spite of tremendous physical limitations. One is reminded through Harlan's story of what is really important in life: a loving supportive family, faith in the living God, and a spirit of determination and attitude of never giving up.

We all want things to be perfect in life but the reality is that they almost never are in this fallen world. Human nature would look at a cerebral palsy child who will never walk and needs help with most common task of daily living and think of it as a grievous misfortune. Expectations for much to ever become of someone with such limitations would be a common response. Harlan's story will inspire you to think differently as you read about a life that has been so full. Full of such a wide range of experiences, full of loving relationships, and full of faith in the God he loves so dearly.

Harlan has been one of my dearest friends for almost fifty years. As you read his story I believe you will be inspired and encouraged as I have been so many, many times over these many years.

Roy Peters

CONTENTS

"Before I formed you in the womb I knew you, before you were born I set you apart;"

JEREMIAH 1:5

ONE

UNCERTAIN TIMES

The year I was born, 1943, my parents, Arleigh and Sophie Temple, didn't experience much in the way of lavish living. This entire region had recently come through South Dakota's Dust Bowl days, which barely ended before 1939 brought World War II. In 1943, both Ford and General Motors had switched from making cars to manufacturing bombs and aircraft engines to assist in World War II. That same year, my parents and all Americans experienced rationing of meat, cheese, canned fish, and canned milk. For farmers like Dad, tractors and most farm equipment had to be ordered months before its manufacture.

While farmers in South Dakota had experienced some relief from extreme drought in the early 1940s, most of America still struggled economically. Bank tellers brought home an average of 92.5 cents per hour, and those hiring out to farmers were paid around $1.55 per day at best.

In 1943, my father, Arleigh Temple, was diligently tending to his crops of corn, oats (and later soybeans). On the farm he rented near Davis, he and my mother also milked cows and raised chickens and hogs. Mom always helped with milking, and chicken chores were her responsibility. I remember that their brief experience with raising sheep ended quickly after a sheep pulled the hose off a fuel tank, which caused all the fuel to spill out onto the ground.

As if life in 1943 wasn't challenging enough, World War II dragged on. Men as old as 39 were called into military service. Dad was well aware that he could be drafted and be away from the farm and his young family for up to two years. At that same time, he was offered the opportunity to rent or buy half a section of land northwest of Tea. With the threat of being drafted on the horizon, Dad turned the offer down. Fortunately, the Army never called his name, and he wasn't drafted.

As a kid, Dad learned patience and kindness, traits that served him well. Due to his gentle nature, I can easily imagine that Dad was also preoccupied with the pending birth of his second child.

The ardent devotion that led Dad to marry my mother on October 8, 1940, hadn't waned (and over 72 years of marriage never would). He and his father-in-law worked together well, often doing butchering for neighbors. However, my birth on December 6, 1943, would test my family's faith, commitment, and devotion for the remainder of our lives.

My sister Ardyth (Ardie) was born without incident in 1941, at what was then Sioux Valley Hospital in nearby Sioux Falls. At the time of my birth, my parents chose to have the physician, Dr. Volin, and a midwife, Mrs. Kuehlemeyer, at a house just off Main Street in Lennox. I came to know Dr. Volin, a man small in stature, as a kind and caring person. As a young kid, I had a lot of earaches and they often flared up during the evening. If I needed medical attention after hours for something like that, Dad could take me to Dr. Volin's house to pick up a prescription or get a penicillin shot.

It's important to know that both Mom and Dad had great faith in God, trusting and looking to Him most every situation in their life. More than likely, when Dr. Volin cautioned Mom that I was coming breach, being born feet-first instead of head-first, that detail didn't strike her as anything to be concerned about.

What my parents wouldn't realize for some time was that I was probably injured when I was born. Breech birth can affect the blood flow during the birth process and cause brain damage. It's also possible during a breech delivery that the umbilical cord becomes entangled around the baby's neck. The injury often results in the development of neurological disorders such as cerebral palsy (CP).

CP affects the cerebellum, the brain region, having to do with motor skills, movement, and balance. Damage to this area can affect a person's eyes and various joints and cause muscle stiffness. Some affected people can walk, some need assistance. In addition to epilepsy, blindness, or deafness, CP can also result in intellectual disabilities. In light of that knowledge, I know I have been blessed in many ways.

For the first months of my life, my parents didn't recognize any sign of trouble in my development. I wasn't doing things as early as Ardie had, but children all develop at a different pace. It appeared God had blessed them with a son, and they now had two beautiful children to round out their young family.

By the time I was approaching my first birthday, my parents realized I wasn't doing some things common to children my age. I wasn't crawling or sitting up by myself.

It was apparent that I was far less mobile than "normal." My thighs and knees were always pressed together, slightly crossed, causing my feet to awkwardly point away from my body. It was also easy to see that I was smaller than other children my age.

For a few weeks, the physical demands of farming delayed their plan to take me to a doctor. But by early 1945, my parents and I were in the doctor's office.

Physicians in those days didn't have the same tools nor nearly as much medical knowledge as physicians have today. However, the diagnosis was quickly pronounced: cerebral palsy.

The term meant little to my parents. They had no experience with any other family or any other children with this disorder. But that would change for all of us.

If the diagnosis induced tension and stress for my parents, I never saw a hint of it. I know how fervently my parents prayed over many aspects of their lives, and I have to believe they spent even more time on their knees after that doctor's visit.

It's not likely that they fully grasped all the ramifications of what they had just learned. Unlike today, they didn't have any support groups to turn to. Even general medical information wasn't readily available to any average person, As I look back, I have to believe that their faith in God and generous loving hearts were invaluable gifts from God to me and my entire family.

I was probably about one year old when this portrait was taken.

Of course, from little on, my daily routine was much different than that of my sister, Ardie.

We lived in a traditional, two-story farmhouse. But unlike my sister and most kids who grew up on the farm, my bedroom was downstairs. That made it far easier for my parents to help me get up every morning and put me to bed at night. Typically, Mom got me up in the morning and Dad put me to bed.

Every morning Mom helped me get up and dress while Dad finished the morning chores. She washed me up, brushed my teeth, combed my hair, and helped me with every task necessary for me to be ready to face the day.

When it came time for me to start attending elementary school, our parents took us each day, or we rode with a neighbor.

For the two years that I went to high school in Lennox, I rode the school bus. We had a short driveway, so the bus came right into the yard.

By the time the school bus arrived at 7:20 a.m., my parents had finished their milking chores and had me up, dressed, fed, and ready for the day.

Since I couldn't walk out to the bus, Dad carried me out, took me onto the bus, and set me in a seat right behind the bus driver. Our very kind bus driver, Rients Van Buren, took my wheelchair to the back of the bus, then continued along the bus route. When we arrived at school, Rients took the wheelchair out of the back of the bus, helped me get into the chair, then wheeled me into the school. When the school day was over, Dad usually met the bus, came in and picked me up, helped me get into my wheelchair and into the house. If Dad wasn't there, Rients helped me get off the bus and into the house.

In my advancing years, I sometimes think about all the sacrifices my parents made in taking care of me. When I was old enough to drive a car and go places with my friends, it was Dad who got up in the middle of the night and met me after I drove into our yard. In the last years of my twenties, it was often after midnight when I got home. Dad got out of bed, came out of the house, helped me get

I will always remember the kindness that our bus driver, Rients Van Buren, showed to me during the two years that I rode the school bus to attend Lennox High School.

out of the car, into the house, and get ready for bed. If for some reason they didn't hear me drive in, I waited about 10 minutes, then honked the horn to alert them. Neither he nor Mom ever complained about the extra care I required. At least I never heard or saw it.

Once you know about some of the challenges Dad faced as he was growing up, it's easy to understand how he acquired such a tender heart.

For my Dad, family was at the heart of his life. He was born on

September 22, 1916, on a farm just three-quarters of a mile from where we now live. When I sit in our sun-room, I can look across the landscape and see the trees that still stand on that farm.

Dad's own family was shattered with his father's death when Dad was about four and a half. I believe Grandpa Temple succumbed to tuberculosis, which was quite prevalent in our state during that time. When his father died, Dad and his family lived on the farm where Dad was born. His father, John, passed away in April 1920, and his mother, Ella, married widower Enno Stratmeyer the following February. In those times, when families were large and daily life demanded much physical labor, a marriage of convenience was common. It was often a matter of survival.

Dad didn't fit well into the blended family that included five Stratmeyer children. He felt very much like an outsider. The children struggled to get along with one another, and Dad's young life quickly became complicated. Aunts and uncles made efforts to help by boarding him in their homes. He rotated from one home to another. In time, one aunt and uncle, Lena and George Symens, lost their heart to my Dad. They felt led to adopt him into their own family. However, when they approached his mother, Ella, she couldn't bring herself to agree to the adoption. Despite that, Dad lived with Lena and George off and on.

Joy, Lena and George's daughter, and Dad had measles at the same time. Joy was just three, and Dad was 11. They were both confined to a dark room while they recovered, a recommended practice in that day. Years later, Joy shared her memory of Dad rocking her while she was sick. Dad comforted her even though he too was ill. His tender heart was evident even at that early age.

Dad's mother had two girls after she remarried, Ida and Angeline, and Dad had a close relationship with them. They always referred to each other as "brother and sister," with no mention of being half-brother and sister.

Dad was probably 15 when he struck out on his own, working for farmers who provided room and board as part of his monthly pay.

My mother, Sophia (Sophie) Schmidt, was a spunky one. People said she never sat still very long. The oldest of four children, she was very outgoing and took every opportunity to go to area dances. Her brother George was four years younger, Pearl was eight years younger, and Jeanette was ten years younger than Mom. As far as I know, Mom and Dad met at a roller-skating rink at Wall Lake, South Dakota. In the beginning, she wasn't at all interested in Dad. But he was smitten and persistent. She soon realized that Arleigh wasn't much interested in dancing, but he was passionate about cowboy movies. Mom was willing to compromise and take in the movies, too.

In the early years of my parent's marriage, Dad probably didn't consider purchasing a farm since he didn't have the finances to pay for it. He and Mom rented several farms before renting and farming east of Davis. The first farm was northwest of Tea, then a farm closer to Davis. That place was continually wet. When Dad tired of farming around ponds and struggling to properly cultivate his corn, he and Mom rented a place four miles southeast of Lennox. That farm had a one-fourth mile long driveway that required a lot of scooping whenever we had heavy snow.

After 16 years there, we moved four miles northeast of Davis, which is just a half-mile east of the farm Dad and Mom purchased (a story in itself), which is where my wife Rita and I now live.

When Ardie and I were young, we thought nothing of seeing our parents kiss. They often kissed each other in our presence. We had friends who, evidently, didn't experience that kind of open affection in their family. We didn't realize it at the time, but we were fortunate that our parents weren't afraid to show their appreciation for one another.

"They kiss in front of you?" Our friends seemed genuinely surprised at what we accepted as an everyday occurrence. I vividly recall that Dad often sat in the kitchen, while Mom raced around to prepare a meal and put it on the table. It wasn't unusual for him to slip his arm around her and pull her onto his lap. "You can slow down," he'd tell her as he hugged her close.

That's not to say that our family didn't ever have spats, like every other family. There was a lot of love, seasoned with appropriate discipline. But overall, God blessed our home with peace and harmony.

Among my fondest memories of my mother is her "chicken hawk" act. In the 1940s and 50s, farm families entertained themselves. My fun-loving mother enjoyed shedding her inhibitions and entertaining us kids from time to time. This "act" was one way she did that. We would howl as Mom ran from room to room, flapping her wings and making like a chicken hawk. She even jumped up on the davenport and from chair to chair.

"Now, Mom," Dad would say. "You're going to hurt yourself if you don't stop that!" But Mom kept on going. There were times when my friends came over for a visit, and I'd ask Mom to do the "chicken hawk" act.

"Honestly! No!" she'd tell me. However, there were a few rare times when she did it for a couple of very close friends. But for the most part, she intended her silliness to entertain her own family.

I've shared these details about my family and my parents because it clearly illustrates their loving, supportive nature and the faith they had in God. It also helps explain how and why they provided so much of what we needed in our early lives: hope, patience, loving support, and much courage. Over the years, all these attributes proved to be key to the success I've found at every stage of my life.

Since I've never known life without physical restrictions, I've never really struggled with feelings of being shortchanged or cheated out of something. As a youngster, I didn't realize I was handicapped because my parents never said, "No, you can't do that. You're handicapped." They always stood behind me when I tackled a new activity.

There have been times when I've watched people walk and wonder how they're able to maintain their balance because I never had the ability to walk. And I know I would love to dance. When I watch people dancing, it looks like it would be so much fun. Even though I'm not able to dance like most other people, I dance with my wheelchair and make the most of the abilities God gave me. In fact, during a fast-moving song my wheelchair automatically gravitates toward the dance floor. I can't just sit on the sideline.

One characteristic of mine that might surprise people is my vanity when it comes to how I dress. I'm fussy about being appropriately dressed and making sure my clothes fit well and make me look my best. My hair must be combed "perfectly." There's something about being well dressed that makes me feel good, and I know I'm not the only one with that attitude. I will confess that my obsession with this has occasionally led to the comment, "Harlan, you're not a mannequin."

Like most people, I've learned many things over the years. One fundamental truth in my life is that faith, hope, and love can conquer many of life's challenges. I thank God every day for the faithful, loving people he has continually brought into my life.

"For we are God's masterpiece. He has created us anew in Christ Jesus, so we can do the good things he planned for us long ago."
- Ephesians 2:10

Arleigh and Sophie's wedding
photo, taken October 8, 1940.

*"And we know that
in all things
God works for the
good of those who
love him, who have
been called according
to his purpose."*

ROMANS 8:28

TWO

THE EARLY YEARS

Day by day, my parents learned what my physical condition would require for all of us. The first realization: cerebral palsy (CP) cannot be reversed. The damage to the brain is permanent. However, CP can be managed. Needless to say, the earlier the better, which is now standard practice.

The muscles responsible for bringing my thighs together remained contracted, causing my knees and thighs to press together. This condition is known as "scissoring gait" and is common when motor impairments predominantly affect the legs.

If this condition is not managed, it can lead to the risk of falling, pressure sores where the legs/thighs rub together, and limited range of motion. It could also result in pain due to constant muscle tightness and strain on the joints. Most likely, the ability to walk will be lost.

While modern-day treatments may be different, my doctors recommended a series of surgeries that would cut the overactive nerve fibers that cause the muscles to contract. Surgery didn't give me the ability to walk, but I could be more mobile than I might otherwise have been.

I am grateful that my parents agreed to the surgeries. In that day, it was common practice for families who had disabled children to send them to facilities where professional care and accommodations were available. While the intentions may have been noble, both the children and their families lost the opportunity to find ways to adapt to everyday life. No one would have found fault with my parents if they had avoided the struggle of all the cost and time involved with my multiple surgeries. Many families would have perceived that investment as a loss since the surgeries wouldn't "cure" me.

I was about two-and-a-half when this picture was taken in 1947 at Colton, South Dakota, at the home of my mother's Aunt Jennie Stratmeyer.

I'm equally grateful that my family treated me like any other kid. The only difference between me and my sister Ardie was my requirement for additional physical care. I was disciplined just as Ardie was (although she probably didn't require as much discipline as I did). And I was never excluded from family gatherings or outings. I was just one of the kids. That all says many remarkable things about my parents, who never failed to give us kids all the love we ever needed.

This photo was taken at our home on December 6, 1947. We were celebrating my fourth birthday. Bert Poppinga made the rocking horse.

15

It was probably sometime in 1948, when I was
around five, that this photo of me with my "farm set"
was taken. It's easy to see that, even at that
young age, farming was in my blood.

I was never told that I was handicapped or couldn't do this or that because of my physical limitations. A lot of the time I didn't realize I was handicapped. My parents never dwelt on that, which was a very positive thing for me.

Ardie tells me that I often received gifts of boxed chocolates and other treats when I was young. For some reason, she says, I always wanted to save the present, put it away for a "special day." My tendency to delay gratification greatly irritated Ardie, who had a sweet tooth.

"By the time you were finally ready to open the candy and share it, it wasn't good anymore," Ardie tells me. Despite our moments of typical sibling rivalry, Ardie and I have remained very close all our lives.

Throughout my life so many people have stepped up to help me live a "normal" life. Bert Poppinga, my Aunt Laura's father, built this frame that I used when I was outside so I could stand up. I was about four years old when this photo was taken.

The four surgeries I required as a youngster must have put a great deal of pressure on my parents. We had to travel to Mayo Clinic in Rochester, Minnesota, and St. Joseph Mercy Hospital in Sioux City, Iowa, for the procedures. In the 1940s, traveling those distances was much more of a challenge than it is now. Being away from the farm for any length of time would have presented its own challenges, too.

Like many other kids in the 1940s and 50s, a rocking horse had a place amongst my toys. This one gave me another way to stand up. I was close to 7 here.

Having four surgeries so close together was physically draining for me. Mom and Dad likely wondered from time to time if they were doing the right thing. As an adult, I now understand and better appreciate the sacrifices they made and the depth of their commitment to giving their son the best possible care according to their ability.

Faith had a lot to do with how my parents approached different aspects of their lives. One of their favorite Bible promises is found in Jeremiah 29:11, which says: "For I know the plans I have for you,' declares the Lord. 'Plans to prosper you and not to harm you, plans to give you hope and a future.'" From the beginning, Mom and Dad turned from the idea that my CP was an accident, a mistake, or a hindrance. They chose to see the challenges it brought to our family as a blessing from God.

I was four when I underwent the first surgery. Each surgery included an extended time of healing. I had to completely heal from one surgery before the next could be done. Every surgery meant my mother was away from the farm for a number of days, which left her chores and the primary care of my older sister up to Dad.

Since Ardie was in school every day, she spent weeknights with Fred and Flora, our neighbors across the road. Each day she went to school with their daughter Sylvia. On weekends she was at home with Dad. Dad orchestrated his day so he could be next to the telephone when Mom called to share the latest information about my procedure.

One clear memory I have of those surgeries was the "horror" of having an ether mask placed over my face. Three surgeries were done at Mayo Clinic in Rochester and one at Sioux City, Iowa. Each time they started administering the sedation, I saw a white horse running around a track.

I vaguely recall driving home from the hospital one time in a snowstorm. Even though Dad was always a pretty calm person, I sensed that both he and Mom were quite tense during that trip.

One other clear memory is the gift Uncle George brought to

In this photo, Ardie was six and I was four (1947).
I love how Mom curled Ardie's hair.

me when I was hospitalized in Sioux City. He gave me a toy cast iron W-D Allis Chalmers tractor that I have kept throughout the years.

My surgery "routine" was repeated until I was six. When all four surgeries were done, a bar held my thighs apart. While the surgeries did improve my posture and balance, my legs were somewhat stiff after the surgeries were finished. I couldn't bend my legs very far.

Because my legs were pretty inflexible, they stuck straight out. Once I had a bar to hold my thighs apart, navigating through doorways and getting in and out of a car was "tricky," to say the least.

In those early years, I didn't have a wheelchair. My family had to carry me wherever we went. By the time I was a couple years old, my parents bought a foldable buggy to help get me around when we went somewhere. We often went to Lennox on Saturday afternoon to shop and visit. While Mom took care of business, Dad and I sat went to the John Deere store. All the surgeries and adapting to changing circumstances each year took a physical toll on my family and me. Still, after the surgeries were over and I didn't have to be hospitalized any longer, I could go to school.

Due to all my hospitalizations, my parents held me back for a year, and I started school at the age of seven. My parents believed it would be to my advantage to be a little older before I started first grade. I could hardly wait to start school at our one-room country school.

Although every member of my family – Mom, Dad, and Ardie – did all they could to take me wherever I needed to go, by age 5 my dependency on them caused me to sometimes feel a bit lonely. I was able to crawl inside the house, but it was a different story when it came to being outside. There were times I lay on the grass or sidewalk and played with our dog, Whitey. My parents did all they could to give me a "normal" childhood experience. As part of that, Dad made a sandbox for me, where I spent a lot of time in the summer. Lord knows how much sand I drug inside with me during that time!

This picture was taken December 6, 1950, my seventh
birthday. It was that same year that I started first grade.

Ardie brought home tales of exciting times at school, but those kinds of experiences were beyond the boundaries of a chair-bound observer. At that stage, I got around the house in a type of office chair that had wheels. It wasn't ideal, but it gave me mobility.

Now, I would be in a one-room country school - Bennett School District 89 in Lincoln County. I would have my own stories to share. Because Ardie was in the same school, she was able to help care for me during the day. She was my closest and dearest confidante. Either Mom, Dad, or one of our neighbors took Ardie and me to school each day. In grade school, I used a walker that helped me get around. During our school Christmas program, I was able to use the walker to stand on stage. One morning, while I was using the walker, I lost my balance and fell forward. I smashed two fingers that day, and the scars are still visible.

This was my first-grade picture taken at Bennett School in 1951 when my teacher was Mrs. Salters.

For the first couple years that I went to school, Ardie pretty much carried me everywhere I needed to go. At the time, neither of us thought anything of that. It was part of the daily routine of our life. Occasionally, Ardie voiced her frustration with my constant requests for help. Now and then, she expressed the idea that her brother was a pain in the butt. I realize now that she was just as much a child as I was at the time. Helping me put plenty of pressure on her, too. Of course, like all siblings, we sometimes bickered.

Still, Ardie was there for me whenever I needed her. Mom surely recognized the extra burdens both Ardie and I faced at school each day. We often discovered a little surprise in our lunch buckets. An unexpected cookie or baked goods that helped brighten our day.

Besides helping me move around the school, Ardie was quick to assist me with things like sharpening my pencils at the sharpener that was well out of my reach. And she wasn't the only one in school who offered a helping hand. Teachers and other students were always willing to assist me when necessary.

For five years, Ardie and I went to the same country school. Without Ardie, I don't believe going to school with all the neighbor kids would have been possible.

In first grade, I experienced my first romantic crush, a cute petite redhead who sat across the aisle from me. Her name was Paulette Hill. We often traded pencils. Over the years, I've occasionally seen Paulette, and we've maintained a friendship.

During those first years of school, a wealth of enthusiasm bubbled up inside me each day, and it sometimes took a wrong turn. Ardie has never allowed me to forget that I once repaid her for her devoted daily care by embarrassing her during a meal at our teacher's house.

Our country schoolteacher, Mrs. Salters, was rather like a grandmother to us kids. Periodically she invited a handful of students to her house for a meal. One of those times it happened to be Halloween. For a number of years, Mrs. Salters had students come over, share a meal, then go trick or treating together. Mother never liked the idea of trick or treating. In that day, some people thought of the practice as a form of begging.

Nevertheless, Ardie and I were among the group of students enjoying a Halloween meal with Mrs. Salters. All of us kids were seated at Mrs. Salters' table, getting ready to eat, when a tiny ant marched across my plate.

"There's a pissant!" I shouted. I was too young to realize that I had used what, in that day, was considered a profane word. I'd heard both my mother and grandmother use this same word to call attention to the ants we occasionally saw in our house. Until that day, I had no idea the term wasn't something I should use in public.

This photo is dated February 1952, my first-grade year.
Students are: Ardie, me (seated), Harly Bruns, Virgil Sinning,
Shirley Sherard, Muriel Sherard, Linda Skie, Barbara Skie,
Doug Skie, Richard Hill, Paulette Hill, Carla Hill,
Glenda Kuper, and Larry Bruns.

Ardie, however, was mortified. She was well aware of my social faux pas. The first thing out of her mouth when we returned home was, "You'll never guess what Harlan said tonight!" From there, she proceeded to describe to mother every detail of the ant incident. We still laugh about it today. At least I do.

In this picture of our school program band, I'm using a walker to stand on the far left side, front row of the photo. Ardie is picutred in the second row, second from the left.

For as many years as I can remember, roller skating was part of my family's life. When I was little, Dad would pick me up and carry me around the rink as he skated. Sometimes he set me on his shoulders and we rolled around the rink. I thought I was pretty big stuff in those moments.

As I've grown older, I've learned to join roller skaters with my wheelchair. In times past, when our church had youth roller skating events, I helped chaperone. It was great fun to fly around the rink in my wheelchair. Sometimes kids would hold onto the back of my

26

chair and skate along with me. Once in a while we played "Crack the Whip" on the skating floor. That usually wasn't allowed at the rinks we went to.

One time, I was asked to leave the rink after playing "Crack the Whip." One of my friends said, "Thanks a lot, Harlan! Now we probably can't even come back here!"

While Ardie and I were still in grade school, our sister Joanie arrived. I remember so well that both Ardie and I were thrilled when we learned that our mother would have another child. We could hardly wait for the baby to be born.

Of course, Ardie wanted a sister, and I was hoping for a brother. It was 92 degrees and a very steamy April day when our youngest sister Joanie was born.

I'll never forget that day because Mom usually came into my room in the mornings to help me get dressed. However, that morning, she had been in labor all night. She was in no condition to assist me or to help Dad with morning chores. Ardie helped get me up and ready for school that morning.

The other thing that was so unusual about that morning was my mother's crying and screaming. That was so unlike her. Typically, she had a high tolerance for pain and discomfort. She would often have migraine headaches that kept her in bed for a full day. Whenever that happened, the house had to be dark, and we kids were instructed to be very quiet and not make any noise to disturb her. After some years, she got over the migraines.

But the morning Joanie was born, Mom was crying out, "Help me!" and letting out little screams of pain, so she must have been in a great deal of discomfort.

Joanie's birth brought a second blessing to my family. It was clear at birth that she had Down Syndrome. A couple of people were concerned about my parents' ability to take care of two special needs children. I am thankful to say that my parents never considered that Joanie would be a burden. They believed with all their heart that if God brought Joanie to our family, he would provide whatever was necessary to care for her.

27

That morning a neighbor came to take Ardie and me to school while Dad took Mom to the hospital. Just as school was dismissing, Dad came to tell us we had a baby sister and that Mom was doing okay. Ardie and I were thrilled, even though I would have loved to have a brother.

I was just 10 when Joanie was born, and Dad hadn't yet had "the talk" with me about the birds and bees. In my naivete, I thought babies came directly from God, a gift of grace. Ardie and I had been praying for another sibling, so it appeared God had answered our prayer. Since I was talking about all of this to Mom, she instructed Dad to take me aside and fill me in about the facts of life. Over the years, I've decided that, to a degree, my 10-year-old self was correct. The birth of a child is straight from God, a true miracle.

Joanie was less than one year old in this photo of her, Harlan, and Ardie taken in 1954.

Little did I know that Joanie's birth in 1954 was just the first of several significant changes that would have a great impact on my life. I was approaching 11 years old and ready for 6th grade.

Ardie's graduation that year from 8th grade was a joyful time for all our family. She was an excellent student, and there was no doubt she had a bright future. What I didn't recognize at the time of her graduation was the fact that I couldn't continue attending the same elementary school once Ardie was no longer there. In that era, there were no resources designed to assist students like me with mobility and all the other needs related to my physical limitations. It would not be possible for teachers and fellow students to accommodate those needs.

When I learned about the solution to this problem, I felt blindsided. My sixth-grade school year was to begin at Crippled Children's Hospital and School (CCHS) in Sioux Falls. I would live there all week and come home on weekends. For a farm kid who loved nothing more than being outside and close to everything common to a farming atmosphere, this sounded nearly like a prison sentence.

Crippled Children's Hospital and School (CCHS) in Sioux Falls, South Dakota, was opened in 1952 through a "citizens' grassroots effort" to establish rehabilitation and education for children recovering from polio. That terrifying disease first began breaking out in the U.S. in 1894 when 132 cases were diagnosed in Vermont. Sporadic outbreaks of polio occurred in the U.S. until 1979 when the last case was diagnosed. In 1949, on World War II's heels, a new U.S. outbreak took place. At that time, children who survived and recovered from polio but were left with physical disabilities didn't return to school because school buildings weren't designed to be accessible for persons with physical handicaps.

In 1952, U.S. polio reported cases peaked at nearly 58,000, with more than 3,000 deaths. As the polio threat declined, youth with other physical limitations were admitted to CCHS.

Before I could grasp what was happening, I found myself at CCHS. It seemed all the lavish love and support of my family had been torn from me in the blink of an eye. Up to this point, every part of my life had happened in concert with my family. They carried me, lifted me, transported me across the farm in a red Radio Flyer coaster wagon, or did whatever it took to get me where I needed to go. Every step of the way, they encouraged me, supported me, helped me learn, picked me up, and set me straight whenever I found myself "off the rails." Now, suddenly, my heart seethed with the pain of being removed from that incredibly loving environment and living in what seemed a cold, sterile existence. I often felt very alone, and so far from the family I adored. It was brutal.

I know now that the CCHS policy of not allowing children to have family visits or return home for the first 30-days was intended to help children like me adjust to being at the facility. I'm sure many of the kids there felt just as I did, like we were in prison.

The first couple of weeks that I was at CCHS, I couldn't eat. I was so homesick I had no appetite. I started losing weight. I'll never forget that feeling of being so lonesome for my family. I didn't learn till years later that I didn't hold out quite long enough. The school and my family were very close to letting me come back home when I finally began adjusting to my new "normal."

It's easier for me now to better understand how I came to reside at CCHS. My parents were doing the best they could. They had no other choice. Still, the emotional pain and unpleasant memories linger, and I have always viewed that time of my life as one of the most challenging things I had to overcome.

It's a good thing I had started adjusting to my new "normal" before I learned that doctors were recommending the use of a hand cast to straighten the wrist, arm, and fingers on my left hand.

My therapists today were horrified to learn that, to straighten my wrist and fingers, doctors put me to sleep, stretched my hand and fingers, then casted my hand that way. For the first 24 to 36 hours, the muscles in my wrist and hand were stretched like crazy. The pain was nearly unbearable. Doctors and therapists today would complete the straightening in much smaller increments.

But there was more medical treatment to come. By the time I

was 12 or 13, doctors recognized that my back was beginning to curve. Because my back muscles didn't (and still don't) receive the message to hold my spine straight, my back is like a free agent, becoming increasingly curved, forming a C-shape.

This can lead to serious compression of the lungs, heart, and internal organs. As the curvature progresses, it also increases potential for developing pneumonia. Eventually, if the curvature is severe enough, it hinders heart function. Doctors would have to organize treatment to help keep my spine as straight as possible as I continued to grow. I also had a pinched nerve in my back.

I would need to undergo a series of body castings that would help my back grow as straight as possible as I aged. The recommended treatment to manage my spine curvature as much as possible was using three or four sets of body casting. The plan was to create a body cast, allow me to do some growing, remove the cast, then start the cycle over.

Doctors predicted I would have to wear a cast from my armpits to my hips for at least four years. Possibly five. Because the cast would add 25 pounds to my weight, it would be even more challenging for my family to help me get around. How can I ever say how thankful I am for my family? My care was never just about me. All of us went through it together.

I found it challenging to agree to the castings. Please don't misunderstand. I am deeply grateful for all the opportunities I've had, and I recognize that many people don't have those same options. However, it took a great deal of prayer and surrender to God, trusting that He would lead the way before we started that daunting journey.

The hand/wrist cast was completed first during my first year at CCHS. By the time I was about 14, doctors began the series of body casts.

I'll never forget what it was like to wear those casts. Each one was heavy. It rested on my hips. Unless I moved carefully, the edges of the cast, scraping against my skin, left miserable sores there and on other parts of my body. To treat the sores, the doctor had to cut out a piece of the cast with a saw. That process was horrifying. Although it never happened, I was always terrified that the saw would pierce the cast and sink into my skin. How painful that would be! If an opening the doctor created wasn't in quite the proper position, which did happen, Dad had to widen the hole with pliers so Mom could reach the sore and put ointment on it.

Of course, wearing the cast definitely reduced my ability to maneuver and kept me from some of my normal activities. In summer, the cast surrounded me like an oven. When the weather was cold, it acted as an ice pack. Because the cast confined my stomach, I had to be careful not to drink too much soda or overeat. If I did, I would throw up. Laying down on a bed made breathing somewhat easier since there wasn't as much pressure from the cast. Once we started with the casts, there was no relief from them until it was over. I recall, once the final cast came off, I could finally drink a whole bottle of my favorite soda: 7-Up. I thought that was grand!

I endured three or four sets of casting. I probably should have had one more because I was still growing when I decided to bring the castings to an end. By the time I had gone through the fourth casting, it felt so wonderful to have it off. I wanted it to be over so I could breathe and eat normally again. Today, I regret that decision. I should have endured just one more cast, because my spine is now significantly curved, posing a threat to my health.

At the time all the casting started, I was beginning to drive our tractor more. Wearing the cast made that doubly challenging. I'm certain God sent angels to watch over me the day the tractor malfunctioned, and I came close to destroying both the tractor and our corn crib.

When I wore the body casts, my clothes didn't fit. I had to have clothes that were two sizes larger. Mom had to shorten all my clothes to keep my pants from covering my feet and shirts from covering my hands.

Before the body casts, it was challenging for my family to manage my weight as I continued to grow. That led to the purchase of my first wheelchair soon after I started attending CCHS. It was a positive development in my life that I desperately needed at the time.

As a kid, I loved the idea of being a cowboy. I rode a horse one time, but it was far too painful for me to extend my legs far enough, and I never rode again.

This photo was taken in September 1956. My sister Joanie
is seated in the wagon in front of me. These calves
were two that I bought and helped Dad raise. When it
came time to sell them, the money was mine. It was a
wonderful feeling to earn some of my own money.

My father, Arleigh, and his parents, Ella Symens Temple and
John M. Temple, Ella and John married January 12, 1912.

*"I can do
all things
through Christ
who gives me
strength."*

PHILLIPIANS 4:13

THREE

ROUGH WATERS

I know the intentions of CCHS staff were to provide the most "home-like" atmosphere that they could. But everyone's home is unique. Families have their own characteristics and no two kids are the same. A facility like CCHS never feels like home to the dozens of kids residing there, no matter how much effort staff members invest. My perception was that we had so many rules and regulations, I could never feel like I was at "home."

Before coming to CCHS, I held out hope that I could attend the school where Uncle George's wife, Laura, was teaching. Their daughters, Cinda and Carolyn, attended school there. But that dream wasn't meant to be.

I'm thankful to know that facilities like CCHS have changed drastically over the years. As a child, I must be honest and say there were times it indeed seemed like a prison.

I remember having a lot of rules and restrictions. If there were encouraging words, I don't recall hearing very many. If I've learned anything over the years, it's the fact that encouragement lifts everyone up and makes us try harder to reach our goals. I once had a therapist at CCHS who tended to be very critical of my attempts to complete my therapy. Another one was very supportive. Guess who helped me most.

Even though I don't have good memories of living at CCHS, my experience there wasn't totally bad. One of my positive recollections is that of meeting Governor Joe Foss.

Joe's daughter Cheryl was also at CCHS when I lived there. She attended classes during the day but didn't reside in a dormitory. Every so often Joe visited Cheryl. If any of us happened to see him in the hall, he always said hello and acknowledged us. I have always respected and admired him for his kindness and courtesy.

My perceptions of living at CCHS were certainly tainted by my unrelenting longing to be at home. However, by the time I completed six long years there, I did make friends with some special people who worked at CCHS. I found them to be very encouraging and supportive. And some of them were just plain fun to be around. You could tell they weren't there just to collect a paycheck.

I know my parents had no other choice than to send me to CCHS if I was to finish school and have regular therapy. And Dad made it clear that I needed to graduate from high school.

"I don't care if you're 35 when you graduate," he told me. "You need an education."

Part of my struggle at CCHS had to do with my own rebellious spirit, especially as I got into my teens. Thankfully, as time went on, I learned to accept life as it was but never liked living at CCHS. Looking back, I still feel those were the most trying six years of my entire life.

After that first 30 days at CCHS, I was allowed to go home on weekends, from Friday evening until Monday morning. I lived for those times when I could be back home. Usually, it was Mom who brought me home and Dad who brought me back. I'm sure Mom had decided that Dad could deal with the unruly Monday morning behavior. Almost without fail I threw temper tantrums on the way back to Sioux Falls. There were times I played sick, hoping I could stay home for at least one more day. That seldom worked.

Not only was I missing my family and struggling with

homesickness. At the same time, I lived at CCHS, I also missed out on daily activities on the farm. I loved being outside and riding on the tractor with Dad. At the age of 14, I was old enough to do some fieldwork, and I dreamed of farming on my own one day.

The CCHS school year wasn't like a regular school year. There were no summers off. Each year students had three three-week vacations when they could go home. The rest of the time, we were in class. This meant I couldn't be involved with summertime farm activities like baling hay and harvesting oats and corn unless it happened to occur when I was home.

My family was close to and regularly interacted with cousins, friends, and neighbors for all my life. It was not at all unusual for neighbor families to drop by in an evening to share some goodies and a delightful time of visiting for adults and playtime for kids. There was no calling or texting to see if someone was home. It was common for my parents to finish chores and supper, then say, "Let's go see Fred and Flora." If Fred and Flora weren't home, we drove to the next neighbor. Other neighbors we saw regularly were Merle and Mary, Francis and Mavis, Myron and Ruth, and Joe and May. All these families lived within a mile or two of our farm. It was a neat era when people frequently gathered to visit.

Whenever someone stopped in at our home, there were baked goodies and coffee and tea. Mom was known to delay serving lunch if she wanted the company to stay for a while. Sometimes we played cards. When it was someone's birthday, we celebrated on that day.

If those visits happened on the weekends while I was home from CCHS, I was able to enjoy them. Otherwise I missed out. Family birthday celebrations had to be done on the weekend while I was home. I didn't miss out on everything, but it was painful to know that all the weekday gatherings went on without me.

Mom once teased me about being such a home kid. She said I'd probably grow up and move far away. "No, Mom. I will always live close to you," I answered. As it turns out, Rita and I never lived more than one-half mile from my parents.

As a kid, I also spent many Saturday mornings at Fred and Flora's home because they had the first television in the neighborhood. I watched cowboy shows like "Gene Autry," "The Lone Ranger," "Roy Rogers," and "The Rifleman," along with Fred. It was a Saturday morning routine that culminated in lunch with Fred and Flora and their family. They always gave me a ride back to my house. On the days that I was home, I took every opportunity I found to express my disappointment and gloom about living at CCHS. When it was time for me to go back each weekend, I raised a fit. I screamed and hollered. I admit I was spoiled. But the pain of going back each week was torturous.

One Monday morning, when Ardie drove me back to Sioux Falls, I threatened to jump out of the car. I was desperate. What could I do to get away from CCHS? Every so often, Ardie reminds me of what a brat I was then. My stunt resulted in her refusal to ever again give me a ride back to CCHS.

Before I came to CCHS, I sometimes felt frustrated with not participating in some of the fun activities our neighborhood kids were doing. I couldn't get up and walk across the room as everyone else did. I had to ask for help, then wait for whatever it was that I needed or wanted. My response to some of these situations probably wasn't much different than any other kid my age.

My dissatisfaction deepened while I was at CCHS. I was hardly the only student there who experienced this same frustration. It didn't take us long to discover a common outlet for our misery: smoking.

Keep in mind that, well into the 1970s, smoking was a widely accepted social practice. Since Dad smoked, and, like most youngsters then, smoking made me feel grown-up and important, I started sneaking some of Dad's cigarettes before I ever left home. I had a spot in the grove of trees that flanked our yard where it seemed I was hidden while I indulged in my newfound habit.

Now, at CCHS, my friends and I found an out-of-the-way spot where we felt safe in lighting up between the shift change of CCHS staff. We weren't allowed to smoke there because it would promote a bad image for the school. But every time we smoked, for a few moments, we were in charge. It felt very empowering. There were several places we could go, including a nearby shopping center, Park Ridge. It was three blocks down the hill from the school. We huddled up behind the building with our cigarettes.

Occasionally someone turned us in, but we were never caught in the act of smoking. If someone did tip off CCHS staff to our shenanigans, we had finished our smokes and were heading back to the CCHS campus by the time they found us. We were pretty sure we had gotten away with our hi-jinks. I'm sure we never smelled like smoke!

In CCHS dorms there were five beds on each side of our room with a nightstand in between each bed. I slept next to a guy named Terry, who also smoked.

Terry's bed and my bed were both next to the windows on that floor. During the evening shift change, about 11:00 at night, Terry and I opened the window in our room and blew smoke out through the screen. We hurriedly puffed away for the few minutes we had, exuding momentary bravado, and reveling in the success of executing our revolt. It didn't take us long to refine our sneaky habit. When we were done, we flushed our cigarette butts down the toilet and used aerosol spray to freshen the air in the bathroom and around our beds.

There were about 12 of us sleeping in that room. Whenever we smoked, the other kids appeared to be sleeping. Surprisingly, none of them ever ratted on us. We never did get caught.

There was only one time a friend and I were caught smoking on CCHS grounds. I was with a friend in a shop building. The nurse who discovered us quickly informed us she would be reporting us to the Principal and, "There will be consequences!"

She did report us, and there were consequences. The Principal laid out a passionate lecture, closing with, "Harlan, I will definitely tell your father what you've done."

I wasn't bothered by that because Dad smoked, and he knew I smoked, too.

41

The next time I was home, Dad said, "Son, I hear you were caught smoking." He always called me either "Butch" or "son. "I admitted I had. He didn't say too much else about it. Even though there was no legal age limit to smoke at the time, I suppose it did look bad to see children smoking when people and donors visited CCHS.

CCHS relied heavily on the donations of private people to pay for the cost of operating the facility. After school hours, it was common for staff to lead groups of people through our residential area on tours that included viewing our dorm rooms. Every time that happened, it made us kids feel like we were on display. It was dehumanizing. It didn't take us long at all to memorize the spiel that each tour group heard. We could have easily given the tours ourselves because we knew the script just about word-for-word.

I'll never forget the comment that "This isn't their home, but we like to make it as much like home as possible."

"If this was my home, I'd run away." I spontaneously murmured the comment before I could stop myself. On top of the stern, disapproving look that immediately came my way, I later received a tough-nosed lecture about minding my manners in public. Afterward, whatever thoughts came to my mind when others were present went unspoken.

In my third year at CCHS, I was beginning to accept that my family had no choice in this matter. I was living at CCHS for my own benefit. I had to be educated. There was no school in my community that was equipped to assist me every day. I received physical therapy at CCHS, too. My family was doing their best to work through the circumstances of my life. It was time for me to recognize that, although life was far from ideal, I was not just surviving. I was learning and growing in many ways. By this time, I knew that the day would come when my circumstances changed and my time at CCHS would end. I believe God honored my decision to make the best of my time there, and he brought it to a close much sooner than I could have imagined.

One of my CCHS high school teachers was George Anderson, a

cool dude. He taught English. I'll never forget that he told us that learning how to dissect a sentence and identify the difference between verbs, nouns, etc., wasn't especially important. So we never studied in-depth noun/verb terminology, which would add to my academic struggles down the road.

This was taken the year I was a junior in high school.

Mr. Anderson was very good to us older boys at CCHS. Some nights, on his own time, he took us to a movie. Afterward, we stopped at a café. Every time we stopped there, Mr. Anderson left his pack of cigarettes and a book of matches on the table. He told us he had to talk to the café manager or someone else. He was always gone long enough, about 15 minutes, so we could each smoke at least one cigarette before his return. Surprisingly, he never got into trouble for this. I will never forget his kindness. He seemed to have a caring heart. More than likely, he understood that it wasn't the best thing for us boys to smoke, but I'm guessing he decided it was something we enjoyed, so he would do what he could to help us.

When a counselor named Larry Brendtro came to CCHS as an orderly, I had no way of knowing he would change my life. When he first worked at CCHS, he was attending Augustana College to complete his counseling degree. I appreciated Larry because he was willing to interact with us kids and seemed to truly relate to us. He sometimes took us swimming in the CCHS swimming pool. It was clear to us that he cared about each one of us and it was fun to be around him.

Since Larry was a native of Lennox, we had an added reason to connect. Larry was well aware that I was unhappy at CCHS, even though by the time he was hired, I had resolved to accept my circumstances and make the most of my life. I actually wanted to quit school once I completed 8th grade, four years after I came to CCHS. But Dad wouldn't allow it.

"I don't care if you're 35 by the time you get your high school diploma," Dad repeated. "You're going to finish high school."

Once Larry completed his counseling degree at Augustana, he was offered a counseling position at CCHS. In my sixth year at CCHS, I was in my sophomore year of high school when Larry approached me.

"How'd you like to go to Lennox High School?" he asked. I stared at him in disbelief.

"Are you joking?" I asked.

44

"Well, you're a local boy from the Lennox area. I thought you might like to finish your education there." Larry explained that he had approached the Lennox High School Superintendent the year before, asking if they would accept me at the school. At that time, the Superintendent told Larry he didn't see how that could work since the school didn't have an elevator or any kind of handicapped-accessible features. Some of the classes were on the building's third floor. Fortunately, Larry tried again when a new Superintendent, Mel Logterman, came the following year.

"The new Superintendent said he didn't see any reason why you couldn't attend at Lennox," Larry said.

I suddenly felt like I was in dreamland. It hadn't been long since I had finally resigned myself to the fact that I would complete two more years at CCHS. Was God going to shorten that time?

I was acquainted with Mel. Our families attended the same church. But I wanted to be sure that this was a genuine opportunity.

"I have a manual wheelchair," I told Larry. "If you're not pulling my leg, I'd love to go to Lennox, but I might need help to get around."

Larry didn't bat an eye as I expressed my concerns. The first thing I knew, I was in study hall at Lennox High School. I was loving every minute of my new environment, but I was nervous about it. I sneaked a look at the door of the classroom. Was I just dreaming all this? Was someone waiting at the entrance to take me back to CCHS? It wasn't a dream. My days at CCHS were completed!

As a high school junior at Lennox, I felt very much accepted by my classmates. Mr. Logterman was an outstanding Superintendent. Everyone was accommodating when I needed to get somewhere, which I thought was fantastic. There was only one incident when an underclassman referred to me as a cripple. A bunch of us were gathered outside the building over a lunch break, having a casual conversation. When this younger student offered his cutting remark, one of my classmates grabbed him by the shirt and slammed him up against the brick building.

"Don't ever let us hear you say that word again," he told the young man. "The next time, you won't get off so easy." He let the kid go. I was impressed with the intense response of my classmates. That young kid never did talk to me again. I had some moments at school when I felt somewhat like an outsider. I grew up in the Lennox area, but I didn't start high school there till I was a junior. All things considered, I have always appreciated the welcome I received from the majority of the students there. Throughout the years, I have only missed one class reunion when I was hospitalized. That day I pushed for the opportunity to leave the hospital and attend the reunion, but that didn't happen.

One of the things that endeared me to my high school classmates is my habit of eating slowly. That meant I needed to get to the cafeteria early enough to finish my meal before going back to class. Every one of my classmates was more than willing to help me be first in line in the lunchroom. Even the girls wanted to get in on that. They usually did an excellent job of getting me down the stairs. However, once in a while, they got the giggles when we were halfway down the steps. That made my ride a little nerve-wracking. But they never dropped me. That didn't happen until the last day of my junior year.

Two boys were helping me down the stairs that day. One took the front of the wheelchair, and one took the back. The guy in front didn't hear the one in the back say, "Hold on a minute. I need to talk to someone." All of a sudden, the wheelchair hit the first step. The guy carrying the front of the chair didn't notice that the one carrying the back of the chair had asked him to hold on a minute. The guy in the back let go of my chair, which caused it to hit the step. At that time, I wasn't wearing a seat belt, and there was no way I could keep from falling over the side of the chair as I tumbled down across the steps.

I fell about three-fourths of the way down the stairs and was knocked unconscious in the process. That was probably a good thing because it caused me to be relaxed as I tumbled the rest of the way down the hard cement steps.

The classmate who had been holding the back of the chair

came flying down the stairs. When I regained consciousness, I was lying on the cold, concrete floor. I opened my eyes, and everything was black. That was frightening.

Of course, the students who were trying to help me get back into my chair felt terrible. They came racing down the steps, shouting, "Are you okay? Are you okay?" The guy who had been holding the front of the chair was still hanging onto it.

"I'm not sure," I answered. The student who'd let go of the back of the chair began chastising the other guy.

"You dumb ____! Why didn't you grab Harlan and let go of the chair?" It didn't take long for my vision to return to normal. I had a headache, of course. But there was no doctor's visit to check on my condition. I can still feel the spot where a knot formed on the back of my head. Within a few minutes, we all recovered our composure and finished the school day, which was the last day of school that year. I'm not sure the school officials even knew this happened, and I never did see a doctor to make sure I hadn't been seriously injured or suffered a concussion.

The only time I ever felt somewhat "left out" at school was at prom time. I asked a girl if she'd go to prom with me. She promised to let me know. By the time she turned me down, it was too late to ask anyone else. While that was disappointing, I still went to the prom dance for a little while. Then I and a friend, who also didn't have a prom date, drove around town for a time.

One fond memory I have of high school social events was the Skip Day trip we took to Minneapolis. Dad volunteered to be one of the drivers. We were going to an Icecapades show during our trip. I expected that to be pretty impressive. I don't recall details about our housing, but I remember we were on the third floor of the building where we stayed when a pillow fight broke out in our room. One of my classmates was sitting on the ledge of an open window when someone threw a pillow at him. It hit him really hard. He started tipping toward the open window. You could hear our collective gasp as we helplessly watched. Fortunately, he grabbed the sides of the window frame and kept himself from falling out the window.

Dad took me to some basketball games and an occasional football game, too. As I've mentioned, smoking was a favorite past time at that point in my life. During lunch hour, some of us headed to the parking lot and piled into a car to indulge in our habit. It wasn't uncommon to see a pillar of smoke coming from one of the cars in the parking lot.

Ken Berringer taught bookkeeping at Lennox. He was also the football coach. I still chuckle about the times when we kids came to class and got him started talking about football to avoid studying bookkeeping for that day. He was happy to talk about the sport, and the first thing we knew, the class was over. Interestingly, that tactic worked several times.

Homework at Lennox was very similar to what I was used to at CCHS. The only difference was that the Lennox homework assignments were longer. They took more time. I also discovered that I was behind in my learning and had to work even harder to keep up with my class. Nearly every weeknight I studied until midnight or 1:00 a.m. I was determined to graduate with my class. It was a lot of work, but it was worth it.

God blessed me with the friendship of a freshman named Arlan Hagena (we're still friends today), who helped me pass Algebra. Without his help, I wouldn't have passed that class. I needed a grade of at least 70% and ended up with a grade of D-minus, which was 73%. It was close! But I was happy. And when I gladly received my high school diploma, there was no documentation of any of the grades I had earned. To this day I don't recall using Algebra even one time in my life.

Predictions were that I wouldn't do well enough to graduate with my class, but I wasn't going to allow that to happen. I was determined to finish high school when the rest of the class did. If they had just listened to me and let me take ag classes instead of Algebra, I would have been fine!

"Harlan, it doesn't make sense to take ag classes. You will never be a farmer." That was the counsel I received from numerous teachers, and I'm still upset about that! I proved them wrong, even though confinement to a wheelchair is probably one of the biggest hurdles a farmer could face. Now I know that, even if I had never been active on the farm, I could have prepared for a career in ag finance or some facet of the farming industry.

At that point in my life, neither I nor my teachers could have envisioned that, not only would I farm, Dad and I would jointly purchase a commercial sized New Holland baler and operate a baling crew.

To this day, I'm so thankful I could attend a "regular" high school. It was a great confidence booster at the time, and the socialization I enjoyed with my peers cannot be replaced.

May 1963, my high school graduation
ceremony, sitting with Roger Musch.

My high school senior graduation
photo taken in 1963.

Rita and me with Ardie and her family.

Me, Ardie, Joanie, Mom and Dad in our later years.

51

*"Consider it pure joy,
my brothers and sisters,
whenever you face
trials of many kinds,
because you know that
the testing of your faith
produces perseverance."*

JAMES 1:2-3

FOUR

FARMING DREAMS

When I was growing up, of all the people who believed I would never be able to be a farmer, Dad wasn't necessarily one of them. He was persistent in encouraging me to at least complete high school first.

Dad quit high school after just six weeks because he lived with his grandparents at that time. His grandmother insisted that he be in the house by 9:00 p.m., which kept him out of any evening school functions. He probably didn't have any encouragement to continue his education since high school in that era wasn't a top priority. I did seriously think of going to college to obtain a counseling degree with a background in farming, a double major. However, circumstances didn't support that path.

Among my earliest remembrances of growing up on the farm are times when Dad took me along while using his tractor. I have always loved the sound of our two-cylinder John Deere, a 1949 Model A. From the beginning, I was fascinated by the tractor and most types of machinery. In no time, I started dreaming of the day when I could drive a tractor myself.

During the years when I played in the sandbox – an opportunity my parents made sure I could enjoy – I had an array of farm toys. At one time I used a pair of gloves that I attached to the sides of my toy tractor, pretending it was my mounted corn picker. The man who came to our farm to shell corn, Menno Plucker, noticed my "imaginary" toy corn picker. A week or so later he brought me a toy single-row, pull-type, New Idea corn picker which I've kept all these years.

Using the toy barns, cattle, fences, tractors, plows, etc. I set and reset a farm that occupied me for hours. It seemed I was really farming on my own. I remember my sister Ardie and Mom commenting that they always had to tiptoe around the living room farm settings I played within the house. They were almost afraid to clean for fear of messing up the arrangement of those toys! I also had some Tonka toys, a popular and hardy toy brand in my era. Clearly, my love for the farm began at an early age.

When it came to chores, I couldn't help with milking or other chores, but I did occasionally help clean out the milking machine teat cups. And I loved being outside around Dad as he worked. He had a rotation system of hay, corn, oats, and, in later years, some soybeans. With milking, pigs, and chickens, the farm was a busy place. Mom was his main chore partner, helping pull weeds in the bean field and picking up rocks across the farm. Mom also did daily chicken chores. During that time, farming was a labor-intensive job, and any helping hand was welcomed.

In the years when my parents threshed oats, I was too young to drive a tractor. One of our neighbors, Merle Sherard, owned a threshing machine and went from neighbor to neighbor threshing their oats crop.

At threshing time, usually midsummer, I rode along with Merle on his Model C International tractor that was used to pull the oats wagon from the threshing machine to the grain bin. I loved riding with him on that tractor, even though it was red. There were five or six neighbors on the threshing run, and each of them came to help thresh at every farm. This gave the bundle haulers a bit of time to rest up before returning to the field for another load. As the number of neighbors in the threshing run declined, the job became much more labor intense. Thankfully, combines soon replaced the threshing machines and the necessary manpower was cut down to two people.

For the days the threshing crew worked at our farm, Mom took a lunch out to them each morning. When she made the trip, she took me along, then parked me somewhere for the rest of the morning while she, Ardie, and usually one of the other neighbor ladies worked to make the noon meal for everybody. I'll always remember the sight of our dining room table loaded with food for everyone who helped with threshing.

Merle used a Model M International to power the threshing machine. When oats harvest was finished at our farm, Merle used the M to pull the threshing machine to the next farm to harvest their oats. If I behaved myself, Mom allowed me to ride along on the M with Merle as he moved the threshing machine to a neighboring farm.

The threshing machine had steel wheels, which made the move a slow ride. That was fine with me! I thought I was big stuff!

In later years, Dad talked about how much he enjoyed threshing time while there was a big crew! Once combines came out, oats harvest became much faster, simpler, and easier. Usually just two people were needed for the job, which also meant a lot less work for my mother and the other women.

Families like us still hired someone to combine our oats until Dad and uncle George brought a combine together. In later years Dad owned his own combine.

By the time I was 12, I was big enough and strong enough to drive the tractor. Dad had to lift me up onto the tractor. I rarely sat down while I drove the tractor. I stood, and Dad put an extension onto the tractor clutch handle, making it easier for me to reach it. When Dad's mounted corn picker was on, he used an extension for the hand clutch. That raised the clutch handle higher so you could reach it without having your hands near the corn picker's moving parts. I still have that extension on both of my A and B John Deere tractors.

One of my first duties with the tractor was dragging the yard to help smooth out any ruts. If it rained before the milk truck came, the big, heavy truck left ruts in the yard and driveway. We wanted to smooth everything out to keep it all in driving condition. Smoothing it out and getting rid of any ruts made it easier for my family to move me across the yard with my coaster wagon and a stroller.

A routine task of mine was lining the tractor up with our stationary Hammer Mill feed grinder so Dad could put a belt on the tractor pulley and use the tractor to power the grinder. If it wasn't lined up perfectly, the belt would slip off. I learned how to do that by watching Dad. Turning the tractor just a bit at an angle worked to keep the belt where it belonged. Dad was patient with me. He could have easily lined it up faster than I could, but he gave me that opportunity to learn, and feel needed.

Generally, once the feed was ground, I would park the wagon before shutting the tractor off. One day, soon after I was put in a body cast (which really restricted my physical movement even more than usual), I had just parked the wagon. Suddenly, the tractor took off like a rocket. I had it in the gear next to road gear. It jerked like I had slammed the clutch into gear. I lost my grip on the steering wheel and fell back into the seat. Thankfully, the seat had a backrest and armrest. Otherwise, I would have flown right off the back. There was no way I could reach the steering wheel.

If it had happened when Dad was ready to pull the pin out of the wagon, it would have run over him. It took off so fast it even dug down into the dirt a bit. Since it was in high gear, the granary quickly came closer and closer.

Dad was in the hog house, checking on sows that were about to farrow. I started yelling and screaming at the top of my lungs. The tractor was headed straight for the alleyway in our granary building. Thankfully, the granary crib was filled with the ear corn we had picked the previous year. That made the structure more solid. Otherwise, the tractor may have done much more damage to the building, Dad, and me.

Just as the front end of the tractor went inside the granary alleyway, Dad jumped up on the tractor, pulled the throttle back, and the tractor stopped as suddenly as it had roared off. The tractor's back wheel had hit the corner of the crib so hard it moved that section of the crib about four inches off the building's foundation. I was terrified!

That incident could have been so tragic. It left me so frightened. Not much scared me but that incident did. I told Dad, "I never want to drive a tractor again! This is not for me!"

My love affair with tractors may have been infectious. This is a picture of me, Ardie's son Kevin, and my sister Joanie, who wasn't so interested in the tractor but loved being in pictures.

That morning Dad didn't say anything about what had happened. When he repaired the clutch, he learned that the clutch facings had overlapped and caused the tractor to take off like a shot. I had no idea at that time that the clutch facings on tractors with a hand clutch needed an occasional inspection. If they were worn and overlapped, the tractor could malfunction. Even if I could have grabbed the tractor clutch, it wouldn't have made any difference. It had to be completely shut off before it would stop. A few days later, when it was time to drag the yard again, Dad came to get me.

"Okay, son," he said. "Let's get you on the tractor so you can drag the yard."

"No, I'm not driving the tractor anymore." The frightful incident was still very fresh in my memory.

"You don't have to worry about that happening again," Dad said. "I fixed the tractor, and it should never run away with you again. You didn't do anything wrong. The tractor malfunctioned, but you need to get back up there again."

Dad wasn't stern about it. He knew very well how frightened I was when the tractor ran away with me. He fully understood I could have been thrown off the tractor during the incident. He might have suffered a much more significant injury than the skinned arm he incurred when he had to jump up on the moving tractor to get it stopped. Dad also knew that, down the road, I would regret not overcoming my fear and doing something I enjoyed so much. He lifted me up onto the tractor, and I drug the yard without any trouble.

Dad was so right about me needing to overcome my fears. Not only was it good for me to feel useful by helping with chores and fieldwork, but the tractors I've driven over my life have taken me to physical and psychological places that I might never have reached any other way.

I'll never forget when Dad and I took the tractor out to the field to cultivate corn with his four-row cultivator. I was 13 or 14 at the time. It was common for me to ride along on the tractor when Dad did fieldwork. That afternoon, when it was about chore time, Dad stopped the tractor at the end of the field.

"Would you like to make a couple rounds by yourself while I do chores?" Dad asked. My mind raced. Really? Could I cultivate by myself?

"Yes, I would love to," I said. Like any 13- or 14-year-old farm boy, I was on cloud nine to think that Dad had enough faith in me to let me cultivate by myself. Dad wouldn't be anywhere close to me. I would be cultivating all by myself! He was trusting that not only was I able to manage the tractor and cultivator, but he was also sure I wouldn't take out the corn with the cultivator.

With the tractor turned around to head back down the field, Dad climbed off and walked home to do chores. Possibly he took a couple of peeks around the grove of trees to make sure things were going as he expected.

Mom always helped Dad with milking and all the other chores. I learned later that, when she came to the barn, she was looking for me.

"Where's Butch?" That's the nickname Dad gave me when I was just over two.

"He's out cultivating. I'll go get him in a little bit." Mom was much more protective than Dad, so she likely struggled with the idea of me being in the field by myself, as most mothers would do. But she didn't protest. By the time Dad came back, I had completed three rounds of cultivating. Wow! I was really doing something important, and it felt great!

Because those older tractors didn't have power steering, I had all I could do to make the turn at each end of the field. Part of that was, with the weight of the cultivator on the front end of the tractor, turning was more difficult. When the cultivator was in the ground, I had no trouble steering it. But when it was out of the ground, it steered hard as you turned at the end of the field. Dad had no problem turning on the ends because he was much stronger than I was and used the tractor brake to aid in the turn.

Dad never stopped on the end before turning, but I had to stop the tractor, then lift the cultivator out of the ground to turn.

One time when I was cultivating, the end of the field was rather soft. That made it even more challenging to turn that tractor around.

That day, Dad was shelling corn. I was far too impatient to sit and wait for him to help me manage the tractor. I wanted to handle the job myself. At the end of one round, I couldn't make the turn because the field was soft, and the front end wanted to slide. If I could have reached the brake pedal, I would have easily made the turn. But the tractor kept going straight ahead, and I realized I couldn't make the turn.

Fortunately, I didn't panic. I knew the creek didn't have much of a bank or much water in it. There was little risk of turning the tractor over by going down the bank. My best option was to go straight through the creek, not to come into it at an angle. Once I descended into the shallow creek, the tractor straightened out, and I could easily turn it around. I got my balance and went straight back up the shallow bank into the cornfield. It was a rather nerve-wracking experience, but I made it. I continued cultivating.

When I started discing, Mom was nervous about having me out there. She'd heard stories about able-bodied people falling off a tractor and being run over with the disc. The first time I used the disc, Dad was away from home, helping a neighbor. He trusted me to get started on the field until he got back home.

During the years I farmed myself, the field cultivator remained my favorite implement, and was my favorite farming task. I also enjoyed plowing, but field cultivating was my favorite task because it left the field level and ready for planting. Even as an adult, when I finished field cultivating, I'd look back at the beautiful seedbed that was now ready for planting. It always gave me a great sense of accomplishment.

As a youngster, being able to operate the tractor and help with the work on the farm really boosted my self-esteem. I felt like I was contributing to our family and a valuable member of my family. Over time Mom was less apprehensive each time Dad helped me take on a new task. She didn't worry nearly so much.

I know my parents were happy that I was enjoying helping with fieldwork. I was always up to a challenge. Even though there were many things I couldn't do, using the tractor and being involved with the farm work gave me a sense of purpose and a feeling of deep satisfaction.

It was especially enjoyable for me when both Dad and I worked together in the field. By the time I was sixteen or seventeen, Dad purchased a John Deere Model B tractor, plow, and two-row cultivator for me. The tractor had a foot-starter, which I couldn't operate. A John Deere mechanic in Lennox, named Clarence, who worked on tractors fashioned a hand starter I could use, which really worked out well.

Before I could drive a car, I used our tractor as transportation when I visited neighbors. One neighbor had a good-looking daughter, Judy, which enticed me to visit every so often. We both went to Lennox high school and rode the school bus together, and she was never surprised to see me drive into the yard with the tractor. Her father wasn't quite as pleased as she was. Judy and I sat on the tractor and visited, and her mother, Helen, almost always brought us some goodies like cookies while I was there. Helen and I shared the same birthday. There were some years when it was my birthday, her family brought a cake to our house, and we celebrated the occasion together.

Other times I went hunting on our property with the tractor. On Sunday afternoons, if I was bored and looking for something to do, I'd take the tractor for a spin. It gave me a chance to be outside, which I loved. It seemed I never tired of experiencing God's creation. I never brought much of anything back while I was hunting. If I managed to see something, I couldn't get the gun up fast enough to shoot it, but I still had fun.

For me, there was nothing better than inhaling that sweet perfume of freshly turned soil and the fragrance of mowed hay. There's something about it, it's difficult to put into words.

As time went on, I often operated the tractor when Dad was busy doing something else or helping a neighbor. Dad worked together and exchanged labor quite often with one of our neighbors. I was in my teens when Dad and I worked in a hayfield that he and my Uncle George farmed together. The field was about seven miles from our home place. George was helping, too. We loaded the bales in the field, and Dad and I were headed back to George's place. Dad was with me on the tractor when we hit a big bump on the road. I bounced up off the tractor platform and came down so hard I sprained my left knee. Dad was able to catch me. I knew my knee hurt, but later that day, I felt that knee giving out when we were picking up the remaining bales. I had no strength in it at all. I knew it meant I would soon be unable to maintain my balance.

I was driving Opa's John Deere model A tractor, which had fenders. Thankfully, I was thinking ahead far enough that I grabbed the clutch and took the tractor out of gear so it would stop. The fenders helped break my fall. As the tractor rolled to a stop, I toppled off. My head hit the ground, and one of my feet struck the tractor platform. Dad and Uncle George were there by the time I hit the ground. I was dusted up a little but not seriously injured. It was a severe scare for all three of us. However, by that point in my life, farming was so ingrained in me I never had one thought of staying off the tractor. And that wouldn't be the last time tractor activities became hazardous for me.

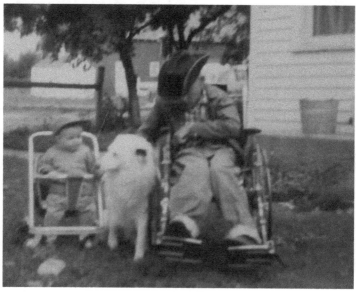

In the 1960s I went through a "cowboy" phase when I dreamed about riding horses like all my western TV heroes. I hung onto the hat for a while, but riding horses never did work out. I'm pictured here with Joanie and our dog, Whitey.

Another time, when Dad and I were hauling our share of oats from a field we farmed together with Uncle George, I was driving our John Deere Model A. Dad was ahead of me with Uncle George's John Deere Model 60. We were both pulling a wagon load of oats behind. I had to throttle my tractor back a little so Dad and I were traveling at the same speed.

At that time, I usually wore a cowboy hat. It was one of my teen phases, dreaming of living the cowboy life. If I had been able-bodied, I'm pretty sure I would have had a horse. I always thought riding a horse would be such a great experience.

In fact, I did ride a horse once at an organized riding event for the disabled. They picked the skinniest horse there, still it nearly killed me to stretch my legs enough to get on it. All the while I sat on the horse my legs hurt like crazy. But I rode. One of my cousins always wanted to find a way for me to ride sidesaddle. But that never happened.

The day I was wearing that cowboy hat, Dad and I were moving down the road at a pretty good pace. For that old Model A John Deere, I was pulling a pretty good load. We were coming up the road on the east side of Interstate 29 (which wasn't officially open then – it was still a gravel road). We reached the overpass that went up and over the interstate. It was a rather steep incline.

On the Model A, if the throttle was backed off a little bit while it was in road gear, the tractor would "prance." In other words, the tractor jumped under the weight of the load. Anytime the tractor pranced, I quickly lost my balance because I couldn't keep my feet secured on the tractor platform.

That day, as we headed up the incline, Dad was in front of me. We had barely started the steep climb when the prancing started. It was too late to give the tractor full throttle so it wouldn't jump. We were about halfway up the incline when I realized I couldn't do anything except hang on for dear life and maneuver that tractor up over the viaduct. If I lost control and the tractor, wagon, and I went down over the side of the road, it was a long drop down onto that interstate. I'm thankful to say that I kept the tractor on the road, and the tractor stopped rocking as we made it to the crest of the hill.

At the top of the viaduct, I was able to throw the clutch out of gear, and the tractor just rolled down to the other side. As I pulled up behind Dad, I could see the frantic look on his face.

He had seen my hat fly off and go sailing behind me as we were heading, coming up onto the viaduct. The hat landed on the north side of the viaduct. My attention had been focused on staying on the tractor and safely crossing the road. I didn't even notice the loss of my hat.

Dad and I were both pretty shook up by the time the A rolled to a stop behind him. Dad ran over to me to make sure I was okay, then retrieved my hat.

"Just sit back and let's have a smoke before we head home," he said, handing me my hat. "We'll take a few minutes here to relax."

As usual, Dad's resolve helped me settle down and continue on our way home. As I look back at it all, I think it was pretty neat that Dad kept his cool, and we were able to help each other get back to business that day.

Dad never said it in so many words, but I believe that his understanding was that God had a plan for my life, and both he and Mom were willing to let me live out that intention. They disciplined me just as they did my sisters, never treating me any differently. It isn't as if there were no guidelines, but they never held tightly on the reigns when it came to living out my dreams. It was one more of the many great blessings God provided for me.

Neither of us ever mentioned the incident to Mom, and we never spoke about it again with each other. For me, it went without saying that, despite the risks, Dad was willing to encourage and trust me. I could hear him saying, "Let's just hang in there and thank God." God was busy that day.

"The angel of the Lord encamps around those who fear Him, and rescues them." – Psalm 34:7

Sometimes, when Dad was in the field, Mom would ask me to help her kill a couple of chickens for supper. When Dad helped, he could cut their heads off, which was the standard way to kill the chicken before cleaning it. I wasn't strong enough to do that, so I had to shoot the chicken. I shot it in the head of course because a shot to the body would ruin the meat.

Chickens move their head a lot, which means you have to be a pretty good marksman to kill one that way. I was waiting for the chickens to settle down a little bit – Mom had just fed them so they would sit more still for me. In the process of shooting a chicken for Mom when a salesperson drove into the yard. As he got out of the car he came right over to me.

"What in the world are you doing?" He was kind of a different person to begin with and it was clear he was concerned about what he saw. Eventually I was able to take the two chickens, and now I have this funny story to share.

By the time we moved to the farm place just east of where we now live, I was 17. With my 1951 Model B John Deere and two-row cultivator, when it was time to plow or cultivate, Dad and I took our tractors and implements to the field. When we worked together, we could get more done.

I thought this was a big deal. To me it was so much fun to work together. If he wasn't cultivating with me, I'd take his four-row. Cultivating always made me tense. If I tipped over a few stalks of corn, I couldn't get off the tractor and stick them back in the dirt. That frustrated me since I'm a very fussy person. It seemed to me that, when someone is handicapped, you have to prove you're as good or better than the next person in doing a task and make sure you're measuring up.

No matter what I was doing in the field, I didn't want to skip even a wee bit of ground if it needed cultivating or discing. If that happened, I turned the tractor around and cleaned up the spot. I didn't want to leave anything undone. My thought was, "Do it right, do it well." That attitude has always stuck with me.

Sometimes Dad would say, "Butch, you're too fussy. This doesn't have to be totally perfect."

My response, "Oh, yes it does."

When I was in my early twenties, Charlie and Loretta Eide moved to the farm across the field, the place where Dad was born. Charlie's father had passed away by then, and he and Dad often worked together to accomplish a farming task. As time went on, Charlie referred to Dad as his "second father."

Generally, Charlie and Loretta were part of our evening neighborhood card-playing gatherings. We got together about once every week to play card games.

One of my fondest memories of Charlie is of the morning lightning struck one of his haystacks, which was in the field right across the road from our farmyard. Of course, the strike set fire to the hay. That same day happened to be Charlie's birthday. For a long time we teased him about having a great big, bright candle for his special day.

I was so thrilled the summer that Charlie asked me to come and rake hay for him while he was milking cows. Getting hay up before rains come can be challenging and evidently Charlie wanted to get his hay baled while it was in good condition. I was so proud to know he trusted me enough to rake his hay. A couple of our neighbors were scared to death that I would come to no good end while operating farm equipment. Charlie's faith in me was a great antidote to that attitude.

In fact, Charlie made the first man-lift for me so I could get on and off the tractor without having someone lift me up or down. I was using a John Deere 3010 at that time. When I purchased my first tractor, a John Deere 4430, he had to totally remake the man-lift to fit that tractor.

We learned that a couple of people in our neighborhood struggled to understand why my parents allowed me to drive a tractor and take the risk of working in the fields. Our pastor let us know that he'd been approached on the subject.

"They can't understand why you allow Butch to drive a tractor by himself when he could fall off and be hurt or killed," Pastor John told us. "I told them I believed the Temple family recognizes Butch's passion for farming, and they thought that if something happened while he was on the tractor, he would be living a full life and have the pleasure of doing something he enjoyed."

Needless to say, some neighbors now thought that both my family and our pastor were crazy! Over time their perception changed as they became more accustomed to it. I actually helped some of those neighbors haul hay and manure from time to time.

The truth of the matter is that anyone can have a serious accident when they're engaged in farming or anything they have a passion for doing. From my and my family's point of view, the sense of accomplishment and self-confidence I gained from helping with the farm work far outweighed the risk that was involved.

These toy farm implements, which I thoroughly
enjoyed playing with as a child, are among the
farm toy collection I have maintained over the years.

"So I commend the enjoyment of life, because there is nothing better for a person under the sun than to eat and drink and be glad. Then joy will accompany them in their toil all the days of the life God has given them under the sun."Å

ECCLESIASTES 8:15

FIVE

YOUTHFUL HI-JINKS

My physical limitations did little to subdue my naturally brave spirit and insatiable curiosity, even as a young child. For as long as I can remember, I have never doubted that adventure and excitement lie just around the next corner or on the far side of the hilltop just in front of me. What a joy it's been, even as a youngster, to encounter kindred spirits seeking similar thrills!

My maternal grandparents, the Schmidts, whom we referred to as Opa (German for grandfather) and Oma (grandmother), lived near Renner, South Dakota, about 40 miles from our farm. After they attended church, Opa and Oma Schmidt often came to our home for Sunday dinner. Once in a while, they were waiting for us when we returned from church services.

For a time, Mom's sister Pearl and her husband Myron Highstreet lived about two miles from Opa and Oma. Uncle Myron worked as a hired man for a nearby dairy. Later in life, he was a cabinet maker. One summer, while I spent a week at Opa and Oma's house, my cousins, Jeannie and her sister Sharon, came over to play.

For some reason, Jeannie disliked her real name – Myra Jean. She insisted that all of us call her Jeannie. Like me, Jeannie was anything but shy and retiring. I soon learned that she shared my love for adventure and didn't hesitate when she had a chance to join me in carrying out a "crazy idea."

I had been using a red Radio Flyer coaster wagon to get around outdoors. That particular day, Opa decided to make a backrest for me so I could sit up more easily and be more comfortable while someone pulled the wagon. His genius gave me a lot more freedom.

Occasionally, when my grandparents came for Sunday dinner, they brought Jeannie with them. She was always cheerful and willing to lend a hand if Mom needed help with dishes, housework, or gardening. As a result, Jeannie became close to my family.

Jeannie must have enjoyed our family, too, because she took every opportunity to spend the day with us. For several summers, while school was out, Jeannie stayed with us.

Even though she wasn't a tall person, Jeannie was strong. As she and I got older and I began running our tractor, Jeannie was strong enough to assist me in a step-by-step process to get up on the tractor. Whenever she could, Jeannie rode on the tractor with me.

In the grove of trees behind our farmhouse, I had a hideaway. I used my BB gun in the grove to shoot at birds, and it was at one sequestered spot that Jeannie and I found we could smoke cigarettes without being discovered. Smoking was a rebellious habit I picked up while I was at Crippled Children's Hospital and School (CCHS). Somehow, lighting up gave me a sense of freedom and control at that age, two things I felt were missing in my life during my six years at CCHS.

While I was at CCHS, Opa would often come and pick me up on Wednesday evenings. His visit helped break up my week at CCHS and gave me some added family interaction, which I missed so desperately at that time. On some occasions, Jeannie rode along with Opa. On the way to Opa and Oma's house, Jeannie and I sat in the front seat of the car talking to Opa. Whenever Jeannie was at our house, she and I had taken up slipping into my hideaway, where she joined me in my smoking pleasures.

At that time, there was no legal age limit for smoking cigarettes. Whenever we were in town, Jeannie could casually slip into the grocery store and purchase our secret vice! If anyone confronted her about buying cigarettes, she used the well-rehearsed spiel every other young kid resorted to: "I'm buying them for my dad."

Legal or not, my mother disapproved of the habit, even though Dad smoked, too. So, it was wise for both Jeannie and me to be secretive about our smoking episodes.

At one point, Dad let me know that Mom was fully aware that Jeannie and I were lighting up regularly. Apparently, Mom could smell the smoke when Jeannie went into the house to help Mom.

"She told me I needed to talk to you about it," he said. "So, I've told you. Mom knows you're smoking." What could Dad really say to me since he was smoking, too?

It seemed that, often, when Opa was bringing me to their farm from CCHS, we stopped at a grocery store along the way. He always said he had to pick up rolls for Oma. When we stopped at a particular grocery store, Opa parked on the side of the building. And it seemed to take him a long time to get what he needed.

At first, Jeannie and I were content to stay in the car and wait for Opa. He knew she and I would be okay for a while, so maybe that was why he didn't rush to get the grocery items.

After this went on for a couple of trips, Jeannie and I started asking each other why he would be in that store for so long just to pick up a couple items. If he was going to be in the store that long, surely Jeannie and I had time to get in a smoke.

"It sure takes a long time to get rolls," Jeannie said.

"Why don't you go in and see if you see him in there. Maybe you can tell what's taking so long."

"What if he sees me?" Jeannie was uneasy about implementing my suggestion.

"Just make something up. Say you wanted something else besides rolls."

Jeannie gave in to my impetuous notion and went into the

store. In no time at all, she was back in the car.

"Opa is nowhere in that store," she said. We were confused. What was going on? It took a while, but we figured out that there was a bar down the street. Opa was visiting the bar, not the grocery store.

We would never confront or snitch on Opa. Oma was well aware that Opa liked to have his "nip." Before long, we realized we could smell alcohol on him when he had a drink. His stop gave us ample time to share a cigarette. If we didn't have cigarettes, Jeannie went into the store and bought a pack. We were going to take advantage of the long break Opa's stop gave us.

After about the third stop at the store, we waited until Opa rounded the corner of the building and was out of sight. Then we lit up the cigarette we always shared and puffed away. One time, we had just started smoking our second cigarette when Opa came back around the corner of the store, headed to the car. Jeannie quickly grabbed our cigarette and, thinking it was out, stashed it in the ashtray. Telltale smoke curled up out of that ashtray for several minutes. Jeannie and I stared at each other. Were we busted? But Opa didn't seem to notice. We had gotten away with smoking once again.

As I got older, I thought Opa must smell cigarette smoke when he came back to the car. He must have noticed that we kept the windows opened a lot when the weather was cool. If he did, he never said a word to us. Obviously, he enjoyed stopping for his nip.

Among the memories of Opa I've always carried are thoughts of his birthdays on July 1. It was tradition for Aunts, Uncles and all the kids to join him and Oma for a watermelon feed. I'm not certain where the melons came from, but we all ate so much melon our stomachs nearly burst. All of us cousins organized a seed-spitting contest and we all enjoyed the angel food cake Oma was famous for making for all our birthdays.

Overall, in the time I shared with Jeannie, we did a lot of fun things together. However, I must admit that some of them were mischievous.

One time, when Jeannie and I were vacationing at Opa and Oma's, we were playing in their barn, a favorite pastime whenever we were there. We were using my coaster wagon to get around the farm, so I was on the barn's main floor, and Jeannie was going up the steps to the hayloft. Suddenly, Jeannie started screaming and tore down the haymow steps. She was so hysterical I couldn't get her to talk to me and tell me what was frightening her.

It didn't take long for me to become terrified and start screaming, too. For all I knew, Jeannie had discovered gypsies in the hayloft. It wasn't uncommon at that time for these vagabond people to sneak onto a farm place and find somewhere – such as a hayloft – to camp out and hide.

Finally, Oma heard all the commotion and came running to the barn. "What in the world is going on? Is someone hurt?" Oma sensed our terror, but she didn't succumb to it. She gathered Jeannie close and did what she could to calm her down. Finally, Jeannie quieted herself long enough to explain what had caused her meltdown.

"At the top of the ladder that leads to the haymow, this giant cat was staring down at me!" Her eyes were still big and round, and her face remained pale.

"Honestly, Jeannie!" I immediately felt so foolish! "We were screaming because of a cat!" It was one more adventure with Jeannie.

Jeannie was about four years younger than me, so she was 12, and I was 16 when I started learning to drive one of our family cars. With all the fun adventures we'd been having, Jeannie was, without a doubt, my trusted companion and partner in crime.

Although I was very anxious to learn how to drive, I knew better than to approach Mom about it. So, I talked to Dad about driving the car. I assured him that, with Jeannie's help, we would be very safe as I learned how to operate our sturdy old 47 Chevy two-door sedan and later our 1953 Chevy. He gave me permission to practice driving on our property.

Of course, I needed help to just get into a car. Thankfully,

Jeannie was strong enough to lift me into the seat.

One day, as I started the Chevy, it started backing up. I thought it was in neutral, but it was actually in reverse. I was headed straight toward our corn crib! Needless to say, I quickly panicked. I would be in so much trouble if that car hit the crib. Thankfully I was able to turn the motor off just before it reached the crib. Now I had to start it again and move it back to the spot where it had been parked so no one would know what I'd done.

Cars in those days had a manual transmission, and to drive, you had to use your feet to work the pedals on the car floor. I couldn't work any of the pedals on the floor, so Jeannie lent a hand. She was in charge of the clutch and the brake. I managed the steering wheel and the throttle.

Dad and I were usually in the thick of picking corn when pheasant season began. The first day of the season was always on a Saturday. Even though it was usually harvest time, Dad and I always stopped picking corn at 11:30 and spent the rest of that first day hunting pheasants.

For several years, Uncle Myron, who was also big on hunting pheasants, came to our farm on the opening day of pheasant season. Jeannie came along. I thought it would be great to pursue one of my favorite pastimes, hunting pheasants while sharpening my driving skills. Jeannie was happy to oblige.

Jeannie and I hadn't traveled far along a gravel road before we came to a seldom-traveled dirt road about one mile south of Davis. In terms of pheasant habitat, that road looked promising. As we turned onto the road, we could see there was a good-sized muddy spot. We looked at each other. "We can do this!" Jeannie nodded to affirm my statement. I gunned the car, our family's 1953 Chevrolet, as much as I could, but we couldn't go quite fast enough to plow through the mud.

It quickly became apparent that we were thoroughly stuck. Jeannie decided it was time to go find help. When she got out of the car, the mud was so deep it almost covered her feet. She had to slowly slog through the boggy mess till she reached drier ground.

Before Jeannie headed toward a nearby farmstead, about one-quarter mile away, I warned her she might encounter an unfriendly dog there. Brave Jeannie! The dog confronted her before she could get to the door of the house. Undaunted, Jeannie gritted her teeth, made it to the porch, and asked the farmer, Bill, to rescue us. He graciously pulled us out of the mud without any problem.

By the time we escaped the mud hole, the car was plastered with mud.

"Looks like you two found some mud," Dad said when we drove into the yard. When he asked what had happened, I shared the story with him. He never mentioned the incident again, except to say to be careful. I doubt Mom ever heard about that adventure either.

That experience had no effect on my enthusiasm to keep driving. Another motoring adventure with Jeannie came when my parents were away from home. Jeannie and I decided to take the '47 Chevy for a drive through our hay meadow. A shallow creek divided the fields. A narrow strip of rock laid down across the creek was intended to provide a solid pathway for crossing from one field to another. One side of the creek was steeper than the other. This inexperienced driver didn't build up enough momentum to finish crossing the creek. As I reached the far side, I just spun out. We would never get out of the situation without help.

"Tell Ardie to bring the tractor and chain," I instructed Jeannie. "And tell her to hurry. I want to get the car back home before Mom and Dad get back."

Faithful Jeannie. She jumped out of the car, walked back to the farm, and rounded up Ardie. In no time at all, I saw them bouncing across the field on the tractor. Ardie did a great job of fastening the log chain to the car's bumper and using the tractor to pull us out to the far side. Then we had to turn around and come back through the creek. I instructed Ardie to stick around with the tractor to make sure we could get the car back across the creek. Fortunately, I gave the car enough gas to get back to where we had started.

Ardie wasn't very pleased with us. She did scold a bit and said that both Jeannie and I were trouble. By the time the folks came home, everything was back in place.

My love of taking charge and traveling around meant Jeannie, and I would have more driving adventures. On one trip, Jeannie and I sped down Interstate 29 shortly before it was officially opened. Another time, as we cruised up and down the Main Street of Lennox, we were both trembling when a police officer pulled up close behind. If he stopped us, surely we would be in trouble. Neither of us had a driver's license. He likely thought Jeannie was my girlfriend because she had to sit close to me to run the brake and the clutch. Even though the law is a bit lax in a rural town, Jeannie and I thought we might be in serious trouble.

We tried to calm our jangled nerves as we carefully turned off onto a side street. Would the policeman follow? What would happen if he stopped us? We quickly turned onto a side street. He didn't follow. He kept driving. We breathed a massive sigh of relief and quickly got out of town.

Ardie, Rita, Melissa Skaff, and me at the beach in Michigan's Holland State Park.

A cousin gathering along with the matriarch of
the family, aunt Ida, seated on the far right!

A gathering with some of Rita's family in summer of 2021.

*"And whatever you do,
whether in word or deed,
do it all in the name of
the Lord Jesus, giving
thanks to God the
Father through him."*

Colossians 3:17

SIX

GOD MAKES A WAY

As I approached graduation from high school, I had considered the possibility of attending college to complete a counseling degree. I had acquired plenty of experience in overcoming my own personal challenges. At the time, though, there weren't many resources available for a wheelchair-bound student. Navigating across a campus and in and out of classrooms would require some assistance.

Of course, working my own farm would have been ideal. But the likelihood that any company would finance a land purchase for me right after I graduated was slim to none. Dad didn't have enough land to support both of us.

Bookkeeping interested me so I contacted some businesses in the Lennox area to see if there was a need for bookkeeping services. That was a dead end. By the time I realized neither college nor a bookkeeping career were in my future, a lawyer in Lennox asked me if I had any interest in selling insurance. I had no knowledge of the insurance business. The lawyer mentioned that he had some knowledge about insurance sales and an extra room in his office building that I could use to get started. I would also answer the phone for him when he was out of the office.

I was somewhat familiar with the lawyer since Ardie had done some after-school secretarial work for him before she graduated from high school. I decided to at least explore my options for operating an insurance agency. I had no other leads on other opportunities. I found that acting as an independent agent was my best option. There were already other insurance agents in the area working for different companies. By setting up an independent agency, I could sell life, health, and crop insurance for different companies that didn't already have an agent in Lennox.

Reginald Wood (who I came to call Woody), Sioux Falls Rehabilitation Services Counselor, was working with me to help with the cost of operating an office and provide the support I needed along the way. Vocational Rehab paid my office rent and I will always be grateful to the lawyer who was instrumental in giving me a start in the insurance business.

There were plenty of times during the process of establishing my business when I needed someone to say I was doing okay and that things were working out as they should. Woody always said, "A client is a person, and you shouldn't lose sight of that." Over time Woody became a close friend.

I was 21 when I got my driver's license for the first time. Before I could even take the driving test, I had to purchase a car and hand controls to modify my vehicle. Through Vocational Rehabilitation I acquired a used pair of hand controls, which are readily available through rehabilitation equipment suppliers.

The first car I purchased was a used 1958 four-door Chevrolet Biscayne. It had a lot zip, which all of my cars did until Rita and I started purchasing vans. A fellow church member, Mel Schoen, financed it for me. He told me he'd finance my vehicle before I even bought one. If I recall, he never charged me interest on the loan, and he forgave my very last payment on it. He was definitely one of the leaders in our church.

My second car was a brand new 1967 Pontiac Tempest with a 327 engine. It was made for speed!

My 1958 four-door Chevrolet Biscayne

My 1967 Pontiac Tempest

Mary Sherard, who had been a neighbor when my family lived in the Lennox area, heard me mention one day that my car was getting older, and it might be time for me to buy a newer one.

"I'll finance it for you," Mary said. "Pick out what you want and we'll set up the payments." I made the deal on the car and talked to Mary about the payments. After I made the first payment to her she told me, "Your car is paid for."

"But I just started making payments," I said.

"That car is yours," was all she said. What a great blessing! Over time Mary also purchased a desk for me that I could use in my insurance office. When I graduated from high school her graduation gift to me was a high-back chair on rollers. She was such a caring person and both she and her husband Mel certainly blessed my life.

The next car I purchased was a used 1972 Buick Electra with a 455 cubic inch engine. It was the biggest engine made in that model, and a tank of a car, very comfortable to ride in. The glasspaks on it really made that car talk! At the time, Rita lived in an apartment on the Main Street of Sioux Falls, nearly downtown. She claimed that, due to the glasspaks, she could hear that car as soon as I reached the south end of town. I think that was literally impossible.

While Rita and I were still dating, I bought a 1977 Chevy van with a lift that helped me get in and out of the van. Rita lifted me to the electric seat, which pivoted so I could slide in. The year Rita and I dated I put 25,000 miles on the van and car, a combination of work miles and driving back and forth to Sioux Falls to see her.

When we purchased our second van, Rita opted not to have a lift. We started using ramps instead, which we still do today. Rita is able to manage the ramps and they have been very helpful in getting me in and out of the van and into someone's house or a business if there aren't too many steps.

I have always enjoyed cars, especially those with speed and power. There are no words to describe what a great sense of independence my vehicles have given me.

I have learned, though, that there are limitations to the power of a vehicle when it comes to driving in snow and ice.

I was in my early 20s when I had an evening planned with friends. It was winter, and that night it was snowing heavily. But I'm young, enthusiastic and feel invincible. I told my parents I was going out for the night.

My parents tried to discourage me and certainly disapproved of me going out into that weather. However, I had promised to pick up my friend's sister at the Sioux Falls airport. I didn't want to back out on him. I'm certain Mom and Dad worried about whether I would make it to my destination.

The longer I drove that night, the more concerned I became, but not enough to turn around and go home. I realized it was a mistake for me to be out. The snow was getting heavy enough I was plowing through snowbanks. When I finally got to my friends' house, I learned that the weather was so bad, his sister's flight had been canceled. I called my parents and told them I would stay there for the night and come home the following afternoon.

I'll always remember the first time I drove to work. I was by myself in the car. My vehicle had an automatic transmission and was modified so I could use my hands to operate the brake and gas pedals. Anyone could have driven my car because the controls were simply modified to be operated with your hands rather than your feet. That first morning it was just me and God. It's not that I was afraid. It just seemed rather unreal that I was tackling the day on my own.

In all the years that I drove to my office, I only went in the ditch two times. One morning Dad was driving behind me. He was on his way to Davis and planned to help me get out of the car and into my office there. There was snow on the road and I'm not certain what caused me to land in the ditch. Maybe I took my eyes off the road or drove too fast.

At any rate, the car acted just like a sled, flying along in the ditch, then taking out two fence posts. I landed in the pasture which Rita and I would eventually own. Dad pulled up to a stop on the road. It was rare for him to get excited, but he was that day.

"Are you okay?" He looked pretty rattled.

"Yes," I assured him.

"I think you can drive over to the gate over there and I can pull you out," he said. My obsessive personality hoped he could quickly pull me out so no one would come along and know about the incident. I didn't want anyone to even think that I shouldn't be driving.

Dad got me back on the road and on my way. On the way to Davis some snow that had stuck on the front end of the car came flying up over the hood. Once we got to Davis, Dad noticed that a staple from one of the fence posts had stuck on the hood. He quickly disposed of it.

We were accustomed to occasional snoopy questions such as, "Does your dad know what time you got home last night?" Or comments about the dangers of having me operate a tractor. We didn't take any of it to heart.

Wally Schiferl and his family have remained close to me and my family over all the years we've known each other.

I first met Greg Schiferl in 1964 when he stopped by my Davis insurance office after school to help me get into my vehicle and drive home. Dad always appreciated Greg for his strong work ethic and how hard he worked at helping us put up hay and haul bales on the quarter of ground we farmed near the Schiferls. If Dad had a baler breakdown in the field, Greg, who always had a knack for working with mechanical things, was quick to step in and offer help in any way he could.

Greg's sisters used to come by my office once in a while. They were gracious in giving my car a good washing and waxing either at my office or at their home.

Greg and I socialized before either of us were married, going to tractor pulls and machinery shows. He gave me my first ride on his 1949 Indian motorcycle. The Indian was a product of America's first motorcycle company, which was established in 1897. I could never drive a motorcycle, but I sure wanted to know what it was like to ride one.

84

One evening, when Greg and I and some other friends were hanging around a friend's house near Lennox, I said, "Hey, let's go for a ride."

Greg wasn't sure what it would take to secure me on the motorcycle, but he decided he would find a way. He had to tie me onto the motorcycle because I didn't have the strength in my arms or legs to simply hang on while he drove.

"We rode all the way to Sioux Falls and back," Greg says. "There were some moments when I wasn't sure I'd keep the motorcycle balanced, but it worked." What a great friend who's willing to do whatever it takes to help you enjoy life!

I first met Greg's soon-to-be-wife, Jan, at her home near Lake Andes. Jan's dad, after having a stroke, was confined to a wheelchair. Greg invited me and Rita to come with him to see Jan as a means of discovering how we might help Jan's father make some minor changes to help him increase mobility.

"I want you to show her dad how much more independent he could be with a power wheelchair," Greg told me. "Especially when he's outside."

Greg had built a ramp for Jan's father to help him get in and out of the house. After being around me for a number of years, Greg was convinced that there were some things that could be done to make life easier for both of Jan's parents.

Sometimes, after having a stroke, people are hesitant to try new things. I spent some time visiting with Jan's father, who couldn't speak after having a stroke, encouraging him, and explaining to him what might help him gain mobility in a wheelchair.

After sharing time with Jan's parents, Greg, Jan, Rita and I headed to nearby Northpoint beach near Fort Randall Dam. We spent the day with them, then headed home after dark. I remember clearly that it was a beautiful evening, with a big bright moon and thousands of stars. It was an incredibly memorable scene.

Of course, it was not at all difficult to love Jan right off the bat. Rita and I were honored to be guests at Jan and Greg's wedding in 1981. It was so pleasant to visit them when their kids were growing up. Such polite and caring young people! Rita and I always got a hug when it was time to go home. And we've attended all four of the kids' graduation parties and three weddings.

What a thrill it was for me to dance with their daughter Sarah at her wedding. She held my hand, and I moved my wheelchair around as we glided around the floor.

Before either of us were married, Greg and I were outside a Sioux Falls bar, getting ready to go home, Greg was fooling around in my wheelchair before he put it in my trunk. While he was sitting in the chair, a drunk came out of the bar. Greg was suddenly inspired to jump up out of the chair and shout, "Look! I'm healed!" That poor guy staggered off, not knowing what to think. It was all good, clean fun.

One time when Rita and I visited Greg and Jan at their home near Fordyce, Nebraska, I was sitting at the kitchen table when I felt my chair moving on its own back from the table. I couldn't figure out what was going on. Turns out that, in their yard, I had rolled through some sheep-head weeds, which have little burrs on them. The burrs were sharp enough to puncture my wheelchair tires and cause them to go flat.

"Now what do I do?" I said. "We're 60 miles from home and I have to get these tires repaired."

That wasn't a problem for Greg. He had a tire repair kit. While Rita, I and Jan visited, Greg went to his shop and fixed my tires. Now all my wheelchairs have solid tires, so I no longer need to be concerned about flat tires.

I've always known him to be a "fixer" kind of person. It was Greg who made the first gun holder that attached to my wheelchair.

When Greg was working in Kearney, Nebraska, we met him along Highway 81. We were headed home after visiting Rita's former in-laws at Plainview. When Greg spied us along the road, he put his brake lights on, so we pulled over to the side of the road. Greg turned around and we had a nice little chat right on Highway 81.

Greg tells me he fondly remembers my mother's cookies, coffee, and lemonade, all of which were served for mid-morning or mid-afternoon snacks whenever we worked in the hayfield.

"And she made the best mashed potatoes," Greg says. "Her noon meals were always so good it was easy to overeat and then struggle to get back to work in the field."

Woody was my South Dakota State Vocational Rehabilitation Counselor with an office in Sioux Falls. He came into the picture when I applied for assistance from Vocational Rehab in acquiring a hand control for my car. Woody and I connected almost immediately when he came to visit me. I could tell right away he was fun, cheerful, positive, and very helpful. After that first meeting, Woody made an effort to organize his weekly route so he was in Davis at lunch time so we could enjoy our sack lunches and a weekly visit.

Woody went well beyond his rehab counselor duties. We have maintained a lifelong friendship. He encouraged me to grow a beard for the Davis Centennial. I've never grown one since.

From there, our friendship continued to grow. Once I had the hand control for my vehicle, Woody and I made a trip to Minneapolis to find me a new wheelchair. I was using a belt-driven chair around the office, which was less than ideal if I had to use it outside of the office. In order to get the chair into the trunk of the car, it had to be partially dismantled. I needed a transportable chair I could fold up and use outside the office. At the time, there was no place in Sioux Falls to buy power chairs.

And yes, I drove to Minneapolis. Woody's superior wasn't sure it was the best idea to have someone with a major handicap drive that far. Once we reached Minneapolis, Woody took the wheel.

When we reached the store we were looking for, I wanted to try out different chairs. I jumped into a chair and Woody jumped into another one. We wanted to see how well they functioned out on the sidewalk, so we took them out the front door and started down the sidewalk. At that point, the store manager became rather nervous and flew out the door after us. Guess he thought we were planning to steal the chairs.

Everything went well, we found the chair I needed, and we enjoyed our trip.

Woody and his family became like a second family to me. As our friendship grew, I spent more and more time with them on evenings and weekends. I recall that their kids, elementary age at the time, tired of helping me with different things. Typical kids!

At mealtime in Woody's house I asked them have me sit anywhere at the table except next to Woody's son Robert because he was always spilling something. We still joke about not wanting to sit next to Rob. It was Rob, too, who liked to jump on the back of my wheelchair when we were going somewhere.

It wasn't unusual for me to go to Woody's house on Friday after work and stay with him and his family until Sunday evening. A few times I traveled with Woody and the family to Missouri to see Woody's grandmother. Grandma Wood was a delightful person. She loved to play cards. In fact she loved it so much she would forget to make supper. Woody had to remind her!

One time, on a long trip, Woody and I traded driving several times. At one gas station we stopped, Woody got out, came and got me, and carried me over to the driver's side of the car. We never thought about the reaction of people who were in the nearby café who were staring out the window. They must have wondered what the heck was going on with us.

Woody also came to the farm and helped me and Dad with a little farm work. When Rita and I started dating, Woody sometimes came along to help me get in and out of the car. We were always telling him to get lost. At times his wife, Linda, came along too. Of course, Woody ended up being Best Man at my wedding and we have continued our friendship throughout the years.

Woody and I loved to joke around with each other. One time, when we were shopping for Valentine cards for our wives, we were having a normal chat. "Hey, how's your sex life?" Woody asked.

"Not worth a damn." We heard the woman as she suddenly walked past us. That's one crazy memory we will never forget.

I kept my one-room office in Lennox for two-and-a-half years. The need for additional space and the fact that I would have less competition in the Davis area was appealing. The lawyer wasn't excited about it. I had been an asset to him while I was there. Even though I appreciated his willingness to provide office space, I knew it was time for me to make a change.

The building I rented in Davis had formerly housed the Post Office, where my great uncle Harm Temple was postmaster. I appreciated that family connection.

TEMPLE INSURANCE AGENCY

It was challenging to rearrange my entire day again, but Davis was/is a small town. I quickly became acquainted with the other businessmen there.

I didn't want my parents to have to come to work with me every day to help me out of the car and into the office. That need brought Wally Schiferl, our postmaster, into my life. The Post Office was now kitty-corner across the street from my office (where the Davis bar is now located). Wally was faithful to come over every morning to help me get out of the vehicle and into the office. There were also Dwight and Lily Anderson, who operated a variety store across the street. Dwight, who also ran a corn-shelling business, periodically helped me out.

It wasn't long before Wally made a two-wheeled lift-like cart he stood me on so he could roll me into the office, then set in my wheelchair for the rest of the day. About 5:00, Wally came over to help me get back in the car.

Within six months of making my move, it was clear I had made a good decision. My business grew significantly. I would later learn that clients were more comfortable coming into my office since I ended my affiliation with the Lennox lawyer. After I'd been gone for about six months, he asked me to return. However, I now had clients that I couldn't keep if I moved out of the Davis area. Regardless of that, I wouldn't have gone back. Things were going well for me in Davis.

Looking back, I would never dream of establishing an agency in the same way. I had zero experience and learned many things through trial and error. Had I worked for another agency for a time and learned the ropes, I would have been more confident and knowledgeable about insurance products and policies. It was probably good that I didn't realize how much I had to learn.

South Dakota's state laws required that, after a maximum of six months of study, I had to pass an exam before acquiring a license to sell insurance in the state. I was studying again! I studied first for the casualty license, then life, then health and so on. Once I obtained a license, I had to learn through trial and error how to operate my agency. I also needed to establish a customer base.

I made many in-person cold calls. At that time, I could drive into a farmyard, honk the car horn, and wait for someone to come out so I could ask if they were interested in insurance coverage. If you did that now, they would probably call the law. I knew many area people, but many were also strangers to me. Nonetheless, I built a good client base.

Insurance industry experts say it takes between five and seven years to build a self-sustaining agency. That is very true! It took me all of seven years to begin seeing some significant profit from my business. If I hadn't been able to keep my feet under my parents' table and live with them during that time, I believe I would have starved to death. They constantly encouraged me. I don't recall one time when they told me I might want to consider finding a different job. Through the struggle it occurred to me that I might need to try a different line of work. I'm so thankful that I stuck it out.

My initial plan was to keep my office in Davis for four or five years, then move to a larger town. In the end, I had an office in Davis for 47 years. As an independent agent, I could find the companies and policies that best suited my customers. That felt good to me. I sold for about 12 different insurance companies.

Flooding was a common occurrence in Davis. In 1984, a major flood brought water right up to our office door. With all the flooding, sandbagging kept the flood water from coming into our office building.

Of course, in 1984 I couldn't resist the opportunity to go fishing right outside the office door.

TEMPLE INSURANCE AGENCY

Jerry Grabow, me, and Patricia Koerner.

I always enjoyed being in the annual Davis Parade.
Riding with me in this picture are Rita and niece Shelley.
Driving my 1949 Model A John Deere is Larry Flannery.

Finding success in my own agency certainly boosted my self-esteem and sense of self-worth. I wasn't just sitting around the house feeling sorry for myself and seeking handouts. I was productive, paying taxes, building a life. Looking back, I recognize many, many ways I was blessed by the grace of God from the beginning and all throughout my career.

After I used the same office in Davis for about 45 years, Parkston's Maxwell & Bowar Agency, Inc. purchased our agency, requesting that I remain as an agent for at least three years. A couple years later, they purchased the building in Lennox where I originally started. When they sold the agency to Jerry Grabow, who still operates the business under the Temple Insurance agency name. Occasionally, Jerry still relies on me as a consultant and mentor, which is fine with me. I jokingly tell Jerry that, if someone insists on seeing me, he shouldn't make the appointment before 1:30 p.m.

I will always fondly remember the many people I came to know and worked with over the 50 plus years I was in business. They were and still are a great joy and blessing for me and Rita. So many memories to be thankful for.

*"He who finds
a wife finds
what is good
and receives favor
from the Lord."*

PROVERBS 18:22

SEVEN

SHE SAID YES!

The first time I met Rita, neither of us could have imagined how intertwined our lives would become. Now, as we look back, we both say God had a plan all along.

"'For I know the plans I have for you,' declares the Lord. 'Plans to prosper you, not to harm you, plans to give you hope and a future.'" - Jeremiah 29:11

Rita's family operated a dairy farm just up the road from Opa and Oma Schmidt's farm two miles northeast of the Renner corner near Renner, South Dakota.

Rita and I were about 10 or 11 years old when she and I, her twin sister Ruth, and her brother Elmer played together on summer afternoons while I enjoyed vacation time with my grandparents.

I'll never forget watching the twins and Elmer herd dairy cows in the road ditch, where the cattle were delighted with the dense green grass. Grazing ditches was a common practice in that day, as was enlisting the kids to "herd" the cows as they snatched up tender green blades with those long, pink, flexible tongues!

The rule was that the kids weren't supposed to allow the cows to graze past the driveway leading into my grandparent's yard. Of course, every so often, the cows, who knew the drill all too well, would sneakily graze past the driveway. Not that the cows were crazy or wild, mostly wily and unwilling to end their green-grass buffet for the morning.

Rita seated, Ruth standing
Twin sisters, five years old

If they knew I was there, Rita, Ruth, and Elmer often ran ahead of the cows, keeping an eye on them while we played in Opa and Oma's yard. Generally, herding chores were finished by noon. Sometimes, after lunch, the kids came back and took me to their place for the afternoon. With my coaster wagon, it was easy for us to travel the three-quarters-of-a-mile to the Bangasser farm. Once there, we entertained ourselves by playing games and snacking on tasty lunches Rita's mother, Mary, prepared for us.

We also went across the road from the Bangasser farm from time to time and played on the country schoolyard swings. The key for the school hung in the building entryway, and there were times that we played inside the school. Rita and all eight of her siblings graduated from that country school. Rita and Ruth were in the last class to graduate there before the school closed. Even Rita's dad Edward and her uncle Francis and aunt Katheryn graduated from that country school. The building was moved to Augustana Heritage Park so we can still visit when we want to.

These idyllic summers went on for a few years. Eventually our lives took different roads, and Rita and I didn't see each other for at least 18 years. When she was 23, Rita married Mervin Weber. His work as a financial officer took him and Rita from Sioux Falls to Saint Paul, Minnesota. There, Mervin worked for a finance office and managed the apartment building where they lived. Rita assisted with managing the apartments and did some babysitting.

After living there nearly three years, Rita's husband returned from work one March afternoon. He wasn't feeling well. Earlier that day, he had seen a doctor, who diagnosed his condition as pleurisy and sent him home. At 3:00 a.m. the following morning, Rita held Mervin in her arms as he experienced an acute heart attack and breathed his last.

To say the least, Rita was devastated by the experience. Their marriage had lasted just short of three years. When she was just 16, Rita lost her mother to a heart attack. Losing her husband in such a traumatic way caused the pain of both losses to weigh heavily on her heart.

Following Mervin's death, Rita returned to South Dakota and lived in Sioux Falls. She helped out on the family farm for a time as she recovered from the shock of her loss. Rita's brother, Paul, managed the farm, and her father still lived on the home place. She was surrounded with much comfort and support as she put her life back together and looked to the future.

By November 1970, that new season of Rita's life led her to work at what was then Sioux Valley Hospital (now Sanford) in the business office.

During this time, I was building up my insurance business, which included providing crop insurance for area farmers. When Opa and Oma retired from farming, Rita's brother Paul rented their land. Each year I scheduled a visit with Paul, Rita's brother Gene, and several other neighbors to review their crop insurance needs. Without fail, I inquired about the Bangasser family. Of course, hearing Rita's story brought pain to my heart.

After some years, it occurred to me that it might be fun to contact Rita and reminisce about old times. By that time, we were both in our early thirties. At that point in my life, I had come a long way regarding dating girls. It had taken counseling to help me gain a sense of self-esteem and membership in a Christian singles organization to help me recognize my own value. In my early twenties, I had a profound sense that I had no right to be married, and no woman would even consider marrying me. My perception was rooted in the fact that I wouldn't be able to help with housework or everyday daily tasks due to my physical impairment. Not only was I limited in those areas, but I also required assistance to get in and out of a vehicle, to get on and off a tractor, and for many ordinary activities.

In addition to the encouragement and prayers many people offered, my wonderful friend Woody, my vocational rehabilitation counselor, recommended that I attend some seminar meetings designed to help people with self-esteem. He believed it would help me see beyond my physical attributes and learn to recognize the many valuable gifts I had to give. I was hesitant to attend, but

I knew I wasn't feeling good about myself when it came to the subject of getting married someday. I simply struggled to maintain a sense of self-worth in that area.

Woody went to at least two sessions with me. At one of those meetings, we were instructed to pair up with someone of the opposite sex and hold their hand. Simple, right? Not for someone like me, whose hands were neither straight nor limber. I immediately balked at the idea of offering my hand to anyone, especially a woman. What did I tell myself? Don't worry; no one will want to hold your hand, anyway. The minute before that exercise began, I reached for my cigarettes (you could smoke anywhere in those days). I was sure smoking would help me relax.

As the group went about finding a person to hold hands with, a lady sat beside me. She gently took my hand, carefully stretched it out, and placed it in her own hand. It was an enjoyable experience. I was elated, terrified, swinging wildly on a roller coaster of emotions. Maybe I was wrong. Maybe there was hope for me.

For one of the last classes, Woody couldn't go with me. I was hesitant about going alone. But the instructor, Karl Schmitzer, was quick to meet me in the parking lot as I arrived and help me get out of the car and into the building. Just his graciousness and kindness were a significant boost for my self-confidence. By the time I worked through all the classes, I had begun believing that, yes, I was okay. Being confined to a wheelchair didn't mean I didn't have a lot to give.

Taking part in that program was a turning point in my life. I came to realize there's much more to life than physical abilities. I joined a Christian singles group that regularly met in different places in Sioux Falls and Inspiration Hills. Through that group and the retreats they held at Inspiration Hills near Canton, South Dakota, I met wonderful people. We all enjoyed each other's company as we learned more about God's word. I discovered some girls were happy to be in my company. Often, in addition to occasional dates, we took part in many different group activities like picnics, retreats, dinner-out, etc. Those were great times for Christian fellowship. It was through that program that I met Donna. Even though her physical mobility had been affected by polio, she was pretty mobile, using crutches to get around.

I had learned to appreciate Donna. I really liked her, and we dated often. But I knew I loved her only as a friend. I had also started seeing Rita more often. Each time I drove to Sibley, 70 miles away, to see Donna, I had an excellent CB radio if I needed any help. We often double-dated, so someone generally rode along with me on the trip.

I always enjoyed my time with Donna. She was fun to be around, and we were able to have some good spiritual discussions. On drives home, there were times when the moon was shining so brightly it made the evening a very special time.

My first "date" with Rita wasn't really a date. I wanted to meet with her and chat about days gone by. One of my best friends, Greg Schiferl, would bring his date and go along with Rita and me. At the last minute, Greg's date was canceled. Being the gentleman and sincere friend he was, Greg said he would still go with me to help me get in and out of the vehicle.

Greg dropped us off at a bar and asked if he could take my car and visit some friends. That was fine with me.

Rita and I sat at a table for the next two-plus hours, barely sipping at the drinks served to us. I don't know how many times the waitress asked if she could bring us another drink. That didn't happen. Rita and I had an enjoyable visit before Greg returned with my car to pick us up. After he helped me get back in the vehicle, Greg asked me to drop him off at his friends' house, which I gladly did. Then I took Rita back to her apartment, where I was pleased to receive a good night kiss.

The reason I explain all of this is that, truthfully, if Greg hadn't agreed to help that night, my first "date" with Rita might never have happened. He is one of many valuable friends God has blessed me with.

At the outset, neither Rita nor I expected to have a serious relationship. After Rita and I started dating on a more regular basis,

Rita came to church with me one Sunday. Afterward, a dear friend of mine, Lila Wheelhouse, came to me and said, "Harlan, that girl is in love with you."

"No, she isn't," I said.

"Yes," Lila repeated. "She is in love with you." I hardly knew what to think. One of my biggest dreams in life, one of my most fervent prayers, was that I would someday be married. Was this real? Was Rita in love with me and "the one" for me?

I would learn later that, for a time, Rita resisted her growing feelings for me. After we saw each other for a while, she told her boss, "I'm falling in love with this guy. I really don't want to. He's confined to a wheelchair."

This was our engagement picture,
taken at Ardie and Erv's house in Michigan.

Like Rita, I wasn't looking for or expecting that she and I would become serious about being together. I was enjoying dating different women and just having fun. I was 33 years old, and I believed that if I was to be married, God would see to it that I found "the one."

As Rita and I became more serious, I knew our relationship was different than any I'd experienced with the other women I had dated. I found it difficult when I finally needed to drive to Sibley to see Donna. It was time to tell her I had fallen in love with someone else and wouldn't be visiting her anymore.

As my relationship with Rita began taking on a more serious nature, I felt it wasn't fair to Donna to simply stop visiting her. Donna and I had dated steadily.

Being the sweet, Christian gal she was, Donna was very gracious when she heard my news. She acknowledged that she had sensed something had changed in our relationship for the last couple of visits. I found it unreal that I had to tell a girlfriend that I had fallen in love with someone else and wouldn't be seeing her anymore. It was somewhat surreal.

"Can we still be friends?" Donna asked.

"Of course."

"I'd like to meet this Rita person," Donna said. "She'd better be a darn good woman!"

Before visiting Donna, I had explained to Rita the need to tell Donna what was happening. Following that final visit, several of us from that Christian group, including Donna, continued gathering at different homes. A couple of us have remained friends over the years.

One of those good friends is Rhonda Riebeling, whom I met through Donna. Rhonda and I always have and continue to enjoy good talks about spiritual issues.

As I look back at those years, I know I was very blessed to become acquainted with and date different women. Without that experience, I believe God knew I would have always wondered if I had found the "right" one. But there was no wondering. As I came to know Rita, there was no question about her being the right person.

A number of those group members we met with were women who didn't have boyfriends, so I was often teased about having a harem. At one gathering, they tried throwing grapes at me to see if I could catch them in my mouth. I managed to capture a couple of the grapes! We had a lot of fun.

After making the visit to Donna, Rita and I began seeing each other on a steady basis. It was clear we were both deeply invested in the relationship. I'm not sure what she saw in me. She may have been surprised at how daring and adventurous I was. But hopefully, she thought I was fun to be around and recognized my loving, caring attitude. I think she realized that, while I dealt with multiple physical limitations, I would always love her to death!

For me, I saw a cute, charming, petite, energetic woman whom I had fallen in love with. My mother possessed those same qualities. I was impressed by Rita's strong work ethic and deep faith in God. She was also a terrific kisser, with kisses sweet as honey.

On many of our first dates, Rita and I either double-dated or had someone along to help me get in and out of the vehicle and get around. It was no surprise to Rita that, if we married, she would fill that role. That might have been intimidating to her initially and perhaps explains why she resisted giving in to her feelings for me. But she soon became comfortable with assisting me and at ease with each task. That meant we no longer needed double dates.

As time went on, I began to know, without any doubt, that Rita was the woman God had chosen for me. In fact, I had a dream about another woman I had dated. In the dream, God instructed me to stop seeing her. I'm so grateful that I took that instruction seriously!

By spring 1977, Rita and I were dating seriously. We saw each other several times each week, and we frequently talked on the phone. Back then calls were long distance, which meant they were expensive. On Tuesday, August 30, at Falls Park in Sioux Falls, I gathered her in my arms and proposed.

Falls Park was one of our favorite places to go in those times, even though it wasn't nearly as developed as it is now. In fact, it wasn't always the safest place to be after dark. Today it is still one of our favorite places to visit.

"Rita, will you marry me? I would love to share the rest of my life with you."

She hedged a bit. "Can I think about it, Harlan?"

"Of course."

By the time we reached her apartment in Sioux Falls, she turned to me and said, "I'm not going to keep you in suspense. My answer is yes." Pull the curtain!

I was on Cloud 9 all the way home! Just a few days before I proposed, my parents and I had planned a trip with my parents to see my sister Ardie and her family in Michigan. I had already asked Rita if she'd like to go along, and she was excited to go. It was just two days before we were to leave on that trip. For several days I nervously thought, "Is this is a good time to propose, before we go?" It was.

Rita and I didn't tell our family right away about our engagement. The night before we were scheduled to leave for Michigan, I asked Rita to come out to Mom and Dad's for supper. She planned to stay at the farm overnight and leave with us for Michigan in the morning.

As usual, Mom was scurrying around the house, packing for the trip, making sure the house was in order before we all left, etc. Dad, Rita, and I were all sitting at the kitchen table. I was waiting for Mom to step in and sit down with us. But she kept racing around.

"Mom? Could you come into the kitchen and sit down with us for a minute? There's something we would like to share with you and Dad."

Mom slipped into a chair, and we shared the news. "Rita and I got engaged a couple nights ago." Smiles beamed across both Mom's and Dad's faces and Joanie was extremely happy. Joanie gave both of us big hugs.

"That is wonderful!" Mom said. And she probably did sit still for about five minutes before she jumped up to finish packing.

My sister Ardie and family knew Rita was traveling with us. I had just said I was bringing my girlfriend along. When we arrived at Ardie and Ervin's home and got out of the van, I took Rita's hand and introduced her to Ardie, Ervin and the family. " This is Rita, my fiancé."

Ardie's eyes lit up. "Did I hear you right? Your fiancé? You're engaged?" They were all surprised and very happy.

That's right." It was a precious moment for Rita and me. "We don't have a ring yet, but it's official." I went on to explain that Rita and I were being very practical. While she had lost her husband, she still had both her engagement and wedding rings. She didn't feel it was necessary to spend a lot of money buying different rings. In the end, I did buy an engagement ring, but it wasn't an expensive one. Before we were married, we purchased wedding bands.

Of course, Rita and I wanted to take marriage counseling. We attended counseling sessions both at my church and hers, a double dose! I attended the Second Reformed Church in Lennox, where I've been a lifetime member. Rita attended church at Saint Joseph Cathedral in Sioux Falls. Through Rita's church, Monsignor McEneaney (Mac) counseled us, and he and I hit it off right away. We were both fine with taking a class each week, and it was fun learning more about each other. It was a great time of growth for both of us.

As part of our wedding ceremony, Rita and I asked Donna if she would consider singing at the wedding. Being the gracious, kind, and caring person she is, Donna said she would be honored to be part of the wedding. We were blessed when she sang and accompanied herself on her guitar.

Just one month before the wedding, we learned that Monsignor Mac had been transferred to another parish. We were saddened to know he wouldn't be part of our joyous day. Rita scurried to find another priest from her home parish, Saint Joseph Cathedral, who would agree to participate in our wedding. We were thankful for

Father Thury, the priest who took Monsignor McEneaney's place.

Not long after our engagement and completing marriage counseling, we set our wedding date for April 7, 1978. Because St. Joseph had so many steps to get up to the altar, we were married at my church in Lennox, where I have been a lifelong member. Pastor Norman Van Manen conducted the wedding ceremony, and a priest from St. Joseph attended the wedding, too. As an aside, neither Rita nor I attempted to convert one another. Over the years, we have attended our respective churches, being involved in both.

On a typical Sunday, Rita drops me off at my church, then goes on to her church, which is just one mile away. If there are Sunday morning conflicts with church events at either congregation, Rita attends her church on Saturday evening, and I occasionally go with her. Rita has always been involved in church activities and functions at both churches. As often as possible, we worship together. Some friends at Rita's church tease me that if food is involved in a church event, they know I'll be there.

My sister Joanie was among Rita's attendants. My niece Debbie was the flower girl and Rita's nephew Terry was the ring bearer. Rita's twin sister Ruth was the Maid of Honor and Rita's niece, Susan, was the third attendant. Joanie, who grew up calling me "Brother" rather than Harlan, was thrilled to be included in the wedding. Joanie was always so short, and wouldn't you know, for marching in she was matched up with my tallest friend, Roy. But that didn't matter at all to Joanie. Weeks before the wedding and throughout that day, she beamed with pride, so honored to participate in our joyful day.

On the day of the wedding, Joanie joined Rita, Ruth, and Susan at the hairdresser. That meant the world to Joanie, to have someone fix her hair.

About a week before the wedding, my close friend Woody (Reginald Wood) volunteered to accompany me throughout the day of the wedding, helping me get ready for the ceremony. Since he was my Best Man, Woody and I both got haircuts that morning, too. He was beside me all day, seeing that I got where I needed to go and making sure I had everything I needed.

My attendants included Woody, my best man, a rehabilitation counselor; Dr. Roy Peters, a veterinarian; and Joel Klusmann, a mortician. I always said I had all my bases covered with a counselor, doctor, and mortician participating in my wedding. I insisted that all of them wear cowboy boots since that's what I wore.

Of course, there had to be some mischief at the wedding. Early that Friday afternoon, Mike Brown, Ardie's son Kevin and daughter Shelley asked for the keys to my car so they could wash it for us.

"We want your car to be clean and shiny," they told me. What they were really up to was filling the trunk with cans that they would flip out of the trunk once Rita and I were ready to leave the church. Their plan worked well, and those cans rattled and clattered behind us then as we made a loop through Lennox and through Davis. The cans did their job, clanging and banging all the way through both communities. A parade of cars followed us through Lennox and to Davis. In Davis, we stopped at the park, where my cousin Patty Sinning and her husband Steve helped Rita toss the cans back into the trunk.

Before the wedding, we got wind of a plan to steal the bride, a traditional practice in our community at that time. We had devised our own plan to set them up to steal Rita's twin sister Ruth instead. We were concerned that Rita's two children may have given it all away if they called out, "Mommy!" as they saw their mother being carried off. None of it ever happened, but it would have been hilarious if all the plans had come together.

Ardie and Woody worked together to get me into my tuxedo before the wedding ceremony. It involved some trying moments, which brought on the giggles for both Ardie and Woody. My vanity, of course, played a role in the process, and there was some short-lived concern about getting me ready in time to get to church. But we made it!

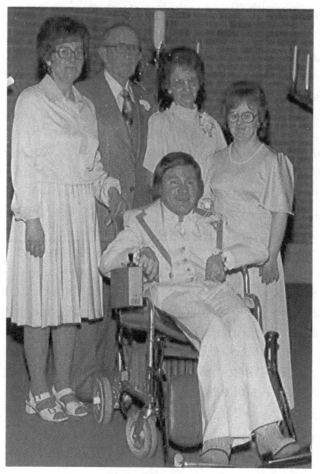

Pictured left to right:
My sister Ardie, my father Arleigh ,
mother Sophie and sister Joanie.

It was very special to me that both my parents walked with me down the aisle that day. For the second time, Rita's father, Edward, walked with her down the aisle.

Ardie and Ervin's neighbors from Michigan, the Browns, attended the wedding. Through visits to Ardie and Ervin, the Browns had become our Michigan family.

Dad and Ervin built a carpeted ramp that sat over the two steps leading up to the church altar. As I approached the ramp, I stopped my chair just at the ramp's edge. That was a bad idea. When I started to move onto the ramp, my wheelchair didn't want to make the jump. I remember hearing Dad say, "Give it heck, son!" Thankfully I made it up the ramp without incident.

As we planned our wedding ceremony, I thought it was important to make the guests feel they were part of the ceremony. My plan, once I got up on the altar, was to turn my chair so Rita and I were facing the congregation and our pastor stood with his back to the congregation. Immediately I realized my plan wasn't a good idea. During rehearsal, no one was sitting in the pews, eyes fastened on us. Looking at everyone who had gathered for the ceremony was a little unnerving.

Rita sat beside me on a white stool. I was sure I'd do something, like drop her ring, before we got through it all. Thank God nothing like that happened.

Pictured left to right: Back row - Ervin and Ardie,
Arleigh and Sophie, Shelley and Kevin.
Robert and Joanie, Harlan, Deborah, and Rita.

Following the wedding, we held a reception in the church social hall. Once the festivities came to a close, Rita and I strolled through a shower of rice as Woody helped get me into the car. We had reserved a room at the Holiday Inn, and Woody offered to meet us to assist with getting into the hotel. I heard later that some of Woody's family members, who lived in Kansas, were visiting that same weekend. They were somewhat unhappy that Woody spent so much time with Rita and me that Friday. However, his assistance was such a blessing to us. We are forever grateful for his generous gift of the day.

Sunday after the wedding, since we were right in Sioux Falls, Rita and I both wanted to attend her home church, St. Joseph's Cathedral. Woody came to our hotel, helped again with getting me into the car, then accompanied us to the Cathedral, joining us for Mass. To this day, we count Woody and his family as one of our closest friends.

Rita's brother, Paul, and his family also attended St. Joseph's Cathedral. After Mass, Paul had to tease us a little bit.

"I saw Woody was in church with you this morning," Paul said. "Did he spend your whole honeymoon with you?"

"Of course not," I said.

Our first honeymoon was brief. We traveled a whole 30 miles to the Sioux Falls downtown Holiday Inn! Several months later we took a two-week trip that took us near Britton, South Dakota, to spend a couple of days with the Symens family. We drove on to Deer River, Minnesota, where Rita's sister,Loretta and family lived. From there we drove into Canada, where we encountered terrible fog.

Every couple of hours Rita and I took turns driving. We were on strange, curvy roads and going up and down a lot of hills. I'm sure we missed seeing some beautiful country.

The first night in Canada we stayed at Thunder Bay, then drove on to Sioux Saint Marie, Michigan, to see the locks. From there we traveled to Holland, Michigan, to visit my sister and her family. We didn't cover as many miles each day as we had planned, which meant we arrived at Ervin and Ardie's home a day later than we expected.

The trip was a fun-filled adventure, then it was time to get back to work. Thankfully, Mom and a friend manned the insurance agency while we were gone.

A couple of weeks after we were married, Rita and I thought we were going to go out for the evening with our friends, Gerald and Diane. They drove into our yard, then one car after another started coming into the driveway after them.

Rita and I panicked, asking each other how we would ever feed so many people. We didn't have to worry. Gerald and Diane were in charge of keeping us home that evening for a shivaree. This event, a noisy celebration of marriage, has been a longtime tradition in our neck of the words.

Wally Schiferl brought his 1924 Model T Ford truck, got Rita and I in the back of the truck, and paraded us through Davis a couple of times. Once we were done driving through town he took us to the park, where family and friends had set up a big feast to help us celebrate. It was a totally unexpected and lovely surprise for us.

It was 1972 when my parents bought the farm where Rita and I have always lived. For the next six years, Mom and Dad continued renting and living at a nearby farm, farming both places. In 1978, they expected to stay on the rented farm until the following spring.

As a wedding present, my parents gave Rita and me an acre of ground on their new farm's building site. A two-story house stood there that was probably at least 100 years old. Remarkably, the first floor of the house was in pretty good condition. Rita and I wouldn't get much use out of the second story anyway. Thankfully, the bathroom was a good size so it was easy for me to maneuver my wheelchair. The living room floor, though, was so slanted that the cart we sat our TV on caught us completely off guard when it suddenly started rolling toward the wall one night.

When we explored the cost of repairing that house's foundation, badly deteriorated roof, and interior, we learned it would take at least $30,000 for the renovation. When we were done, it would still be an old house. It only made sense for all of us to build a new home.

Rita and I planned to live in the old house until we finished building the new one. Mom and Dad planned to continue renting the nearby farm until they completed construction of their new home.

We hadn't been engaged long when Rita and I started planning the design for our new house. We toured six different homes in Sioux Falls that were designed for people in wheelchairs. It was a blessing that these folks were willing to allow us to look over their homes and learn about our design options.

Through the tours we picked up many ideas, things we wouldn't have thought about, that have proven to be beneficial in our own home design. We also worked with an architect and contractor who themselves were disabled and in wheelchairs. They understood our needs and the reason we didn't want any steps in the house, and why the concrete needed to be flush with the house's threshold. Rita's brother, Gene Bangasser, a contractor, was also helpful, acquiring all our appliances at a discounted price.

Initially I applied for an FHA (Farm and Home Association) loan. When I submitted our floor plan, they told us our house design was too large. If we received a loan from FHA, we were only allowed to have a single-stall garage. Clearly that wasn't going to work for me. To get in and out of our van I needed eight feet of open space. FHA agreed to compromise on the space, but were adamant about having just one stall for a vehicle.

As we struggled through all this red tape, a friend asked us if we had checked with Western Bank in Sioux Falls about a first-time-homeowner's loan. Thankfully, we looked into this option.

Our banker was a helpful and fun guy. I'll always remember the day I brought in our blueprints. As he rolled the house plan open, "Oh, my!" he said. "You have done your homework. This looks like a perfect plan."

Our plan included large doorways and a wide hallway that allowed plenty of room for a wheelchair. The bathroom was large enough to easily accommodate a wheelchair, and our 28x28-stall garage left plenty of room for me to get in and out of our van.

My banker didn't hesitate to gather the necessary paperwork to draw up our home loan. It was necessary to secure the loan while I was still single. Once we were married, we wouldn't qualify for this specific loan. The banker loved to tease me about the prospect of postponing the wedding if the loan process was delayed.

"You'll have to be the one to tell Rita about that," I told him. "I have her phone number right here." The banker and I had a good laugh about it. Thankfully I signed the papers two days before our wedding.

Before our wedding, Rita, Mom and Dad, Charles and Loretta Eide, and Vernon and Esther Buse cleaned and painted the entire inside of the old house to spruce and brighten it up before Rita and I moved in.

It was mid-May 1978 when construction of our new home began. It was convenient to be living in the old house, right across the driveway from the site where the new house was going up. We were able to monitor the building progress every day. At the same time, the contractor started building Mom and Dad's new house.

Shortly after construction of the houses began, Mom and Dad were beginning to feel some pressure to move off the rented farm. Their landlord had been remodeling that farmhouse. Now they learned they would have to move as soon as possible.

The news, which rushed them to move, put them in a dilemma. They had no choice but to build their new home sooner than expected.

Since the same contractor was building both our homes, we arranged to have them focus on finishing Mom and Dad's house, then complete ours. When it was all said and done, in October 1978 Mom and Dad moved into their new house.

Rita and I lived in the old house for eight months, moving into our new home right before Thanksgiving. We were thankful to move because, once winter settled in, we quickly learned the old house wasn't well insulated. It was downright cold. The November day we moved out, the water froze up in that old home.

We were only in the new house one day before neighbors and friends held a surprise housewarming for us. Roy Peters was very instrumental in organizing the event as he was home from college at the time and had helped us with our move.

Rita and I should have known something was up that day when Mom insisted that we hang curtains earlier in the day. That really rushed Rita, but she and Mom got the curtains up before 20-some people knocked on our door that evening. Turned out Mom knew all about the party plan.

Even though Rita's first marriage was brief, she remained very close to Mervin's parents and extended family. Needless to say, before Rita and I were married, I was pretty apprehensive about meeting the Webers for the first time. Not having known them before, I sensed I might be a bit like a foreigner in their midst, which could prove to be uncomfortable.

Since her former father-in-law, Millard, was a farmer too, he and I hit it off right away. His wife, Esther, was an excellent cook. While Millard and I got to know each other during that first visit, Esther made a delicious roast beef dinner.

Millard and I were visiting in the parlor while Rita and Esther worked in the kitchen. Later, Rita told me that Esther remarked she couldn't recall a time when Millard visited as much with anyone as he was visiting with me.

I shouldn't have worried. Some members of the Weber family, including Millard and Esther, attended our wedding. Over the years, the Webers have proven to be a great blessing to Rita and me, causing us to feel very much at home in their midst and including us in family celebrations.

People sometimes ask if Rita and I decided not to have children. Actually, we would have been delighted to have children. However, it was not in God's plan. Instead of our own children, God blessed us with godchildren and many nieces and nephews, all of whom have brought great joy into our lives.

The first years we were married, Rita and I had a wonderful Blue

Heeler/Australian Shepherd-cross dog named Dusty. She loved Dad, and since the folks lived so close to us, Dusty went over to visit Dad every morning, except Sunday. Every morning she'd jump into the pickup cab with Dad to ride back to the farm. Those two developed an incredible bond.

By the time Dusty was 15 or 16, her health really started declining. She was becoming incontinent and had great difficulty getting around.

One morning, before I went to work, Rita and I spoke of the need to have the vet come and put Dusty to sleep so she wouldn't have to suffer any longer. But we never had the chance to contact the vet. That same afternoon, Dusty lay down in Rita's flower bed and breathed her last. It was as if she wanted us to know she wanted to leave of her own accord.

I can't emphasize enough how thankful I am that God brought me and Rita together. Rita tells me that she was first attracted to me because of my positive and upbeat attitude. She also liked it that I seemed interested in everyone and everything. I've always been ready to try just about anything that comes my way and I love to encourage others to try new things.

Rita says she was looking for friendship when we started seeing each other. But God had a different plan for us. Love happened, and we firmly believe God was orchestrating all of it. We are both amazed when we look back at the fabric of our lives that God has weaved over the years.

Rita doesn't admit to this, but she was the first one to say, "I love you." Another thing she doesn't like to admit is that I was usually the one who, late in the evening of our dates, said I'd better get going. She would ask, "Can't you hold me a little longer?"

My marriage to Rita has been so much more rewarding than I could ever have imagined. It's difficult to put into words, but I'm eternally grateful that God answered my prayers and played a role in helping me realize my dream of being married to this sweet, sweet gal.

*"And God is able to
bless you abundantly,
so that in all things,
at all times,
having all you need,
you will abound in
every good work."*

2 CORINTHIANS 9:8

EIGHT

My Farming Days!

L ike many farmers, I don't expect to ever stop missing the rewards of preparing and planting fields and harvesting crops. My main goal in life was to operate my tractors, cultivate corn and soybeans and get fields ready for planting. My favorite activities were discing and running the field cultivator. After Dad retired from farming, Rita and I hired help for planting and harvest. Anyone who shares my passion understands my sense of loss.

When I first started driving a tractor, around age 12, I stood up. My legs were stronger then and it was more comfortable for me to drive that way. I could easily reach the throttle on Dad's 1949 John Deere A.

As I got older, I helped Dad with cultivating corn and soybeans and field preparation for planting. Sometimes he allowed me to run the pull-type combine when we harvested oats. Dad never asked me to plant corn. I think he realized the rows might not be very straight, and he was very particular about having straight corn and soybean rows.

Anything I could do then to help operate farm machinery made me happy. I was always eager to learn how to run a different piece of equipment.

When I helped seed oats, I counted the rows so I could thoroughly seed the fields. There were nine rows in each round. Every so often Dad would check in on me and say, "Move over a row to the left," or "Move over a row to the right." Once in a while I was one row off, so I'd go back across that area. I was always happy to finish this job since it was so difficult to tell where you planted the seed.

Using an 18-foot land roller after we planted oats was one of my least favorite jobs. The roller forced seed down into the soil and pushed down small rocks and corn stumps to assist seed-to-soil contact. It was difficult to see where you'd been, especially if the sun was in your eyes. A cloudy day was easier. There were no markers on the roller, and it wasn't unusual for me to go over an area two, even three times because I wasn't sure where I had been.

One time Dad came out to help me get the packer straightened out. "Oh my gosh, son," he told me once. "I don't think a snake could follow this."

The roller we used then was nothing like the ones farmers use today. The last one I used in my farming was fifty feet wide.

Plowing was usually my job. It was common for me to get our fields ready to plant by plowing and discing or field cultivating. Dad followed me with the planter. Generally, he didn't want me to get too far ahead of him because the soil would dry out too much before he could plant the seed.

One year Dad bought a loader for our John Deere A. It came in pieces, and I was so anxious for him to put it together and learn how to use a tractor loader. Assembling the loader went well and I was the first one to use it. It was a trip-bucket design, not a hydraulic loader. When we hauled manure, I usually loaded the spreader while Mom and Dad finished milking. Loading seemed like a great challenge to me at first, but it didn't take long for me to learn how to do it well. After milking was done, Dad took the tractor and spread the manure on the field.

Although some neighbors were wary about having me drive a

tractor, I had some invitations to help haul manure. Often, four or five neighbors worked together to haul manure. If there was more than one of us, we weren't above having a race to load and be first to get out to the field and unload.

Eventually, Dad had two spreaders, so he loaded and we each hauled. One morning, as I was headed back to the cattle yard, I was in the gear next to road gear. Unbeknownst to me, the pin came out of the hitch, causing the manure spreader to come unhooked. Since I didn't realize it happened, the tongue of the manure spreader dropped down and the short end of the PTO became locked behind the tractor draw bar. That caused the tractor to immediately stop. It was if I had trounced on the brakes. I slammed into the steering wheel as the sliding tractor wheels came to a jolting stop. I was totally bewildered until I looked behind me. I'm surprised the torque on the PTO didn't break the PTO shaft. The shaft was slightly bent afterward, but not enough to affect its function.

Dad was pretty puzzled when he saw me come into the cattle yard without the spreader, but it was easy to explain what happened.

That was my most exciting manure-hauling experience, other than learning that I should be upwind whenever I spread manure. No fun to be showered by manure!

The year I graduated from high school, 1963, I started running our corn picker. I had talked to dad about letting me try to run the picker for at least half a day. When he gave his approval, that was a big deal to me. I picked and Dad hauled the corn to the crib to unload the wagon. He used a hydraulic hoist to raise the wagon and dump the load into an elevator that carried it to the crib. Once in a while Opa came out to help.

Usually Dad used the John Deere A to pick corn. I used my John Deere B because it was handier for me. Whichever tractor I used, I always picked in a slower gear than Dad did.

If the weather was cold when we picked corn, Dad put the comforter – a canvas "cab" of sorts – on the tractor. When the comforter was on, the only way I could see over the top of it was to stand up. After several hours in the field, I got tired of standing. To resolve the dilemma, Dad just put part of the comforter on, which gave me some space to look through so I could sit down.

As a kid, I always thought it would be great to pick corn. This picture of Joanie, Opa Schmidt, and me was taken in 1967 during harvest time.

In spring, when Dad took the comforter off, he left the metal railing that held it on the tractor. That gave me something besides the steering wheel that I could hang onto for balance.

Once I proved I could handle the picker, the job was mine. Those days remain some of my favorite memories as we worked together to harvest corn. Mom always made a mid-morning lunch, delicious steaming egg sandwiches. Our dog Chico followed her out to the field where he sat patiently waiting for me to toss him a bite of the sandwich.

When Dad bought a 1961 John Deere Diesel 3010, our neighbor Vernon Buse, a mechanically minded person, rigged up a cylinder I could use to work the clutch. That tractor had power steering and a wide front end, and I didn't need to stand up to see over it. I could sit down.

Another neighbor, Charlie Eide, designed and attached a hydraulic lift to the 3010 JD that helped aid me in getting on and off the tractor.

Harlan driving his Dad's 1961 John Deere Diesel 3010.

With the 3010 I was able to pick corn in a faster gear and the power steering helped out greatly no matter what job we were doing. The tractor was so much faster that I sometimes had to wait for Dad to finish unloading and come back with the empty wagon before I could go back to picking.

On the downside, picking corn without a tractor cab meant all the dirt blew right back at you if the wind was in the right direction. It was also easy to get chaff in your eyes. What a sweet day it was when I invested in a cab for that tractor. It was great to be able to look back at the picker and not worry about getting a face full of chaff.

Of course, no matter which tractor I drove, if I had trouble, I had to sit and wait for Dad to come and help. One year we had just started picking corn. Dad left the picker running while he greased it up. He got too close to the chain that worked the picker elevator. In the blink of an eye, he lost the tip of his little finger. The incident landed him in the emergency room.

I was pretty distraught. How could we finish picking now? Surely Dad would be laid up several days as he healed up from the accident. I didn't realize how tough Dad was. The next day he was ready to get me back up on the tractor and get back to picking. His hand was all bandaged up.

"Dad, are you going to be okay?"

"Oh, yes. I'm fine. I'll just have to be careful not to bump it on anything."

I think that year God was merciful to us. Normally, there was always something that needed repair as we picked. At the very least an ear of corn would catch in the gathering chains, or the clutch would slip. That year we picked 99 loads of corn without one hitch, which meant Dad didn't have to worry about repairing anything. That just never happened before or since.

After I graduated from high school and once I had my insurance business established, I found myself doing most of my farming after work. Since I was a night owl, the late nights didn't bother me. The early mornings did!

I did my best to keep someone in my office during the day if I had to be gone. Mom helped out sometimes and I had a part-time secretary who came in when I needed her.

When my relationship with Rita became serious, I asked if she had any objections to living on a farm. Since she was raised on a dairy farm the question didn't bother her. Later, even though she fed calves and did chicken chores on her family's dairy farm, Rita told me she didn't realize she would be helping farm by pulling calves and doing some of the general farm chores on our farm. Still, she helped out whenever she was needed.

As Rita, I, Mom, and Dad settled into a routine of farming in partnership, Dad and I decided to buy 20 head of bred commercial cows and partner in raising beef. After a few years we transitioned to a registered Simmental herd and soon joined the American Simmental Association (ASA). Through the ASA, with the help of Glenn Muller, Rita, I, and Dad began showing our cattle at various shows and sales.

Our niece, Susan Bangasser (now a registered nurse at a Sioux Falls heart hospital), and her family were very active in 4-H. Susan started using some of our calves for 4-H shows. One of our Simmental heifers was named Harriet. She was definitely a "show quality" animal and Susan began winning first place awards as well as Showmanship awards. Susan and Harriet took First Place in a South Dakota State Fair competition.

Susan won numerous competitions with Harriet.

As Dad got older, Rita and I knew that just the two of us couldn't handle cattle chores like calving on our own, especially during winter. That led us to sell our herd to a neighbor, Glenn Muller. Since Glenn has continued to rent our pasture, we still have the pleasure of watching the cows and calves every spring.

Now if a cow breaks out, we just put in a call to Glenn and say, "Your cattle are out!"

I always enjoyed the baling crew I put together. I had four guys in the crew: two on the rack and two unloading bales. The five of us usually worked at night.

During the time we did custom baling for neighbors, Dad and I used a bale accumulator to help with loading hay.

After a few years of farming together, Dad and I partnered in the purchase of a 226 New Holland baler so we could do custom baling for neighbors. Eventually we bought a pull-behind accumulator that we used for ourselves. It held eight bales before the end gate opened so they could drop onto the ground. We used an attachment on our tractor loader to pick up eight bales at a time and load on a flatbed. That eliminated the need for hiring someone to stack bales.

The baler and accumulator worked pretty smoothly, unless a bale turned crosswise in the accumulator. Then Dad had to get the bales straightened out so we could keep going. Every once in a while, if a bale turned as we approached the end of a windrow, I turned sharp on the end of a windrow so it would fall to the ground. It was easy enough to come back later and pick it up and better than plugging up the accumulator.

For a couple of years Dad and I ran a custom-baling crew. It worked well for me because many farmers wanted to bale at night so the leaves on the forage wouldn't fall off in the heat of the day. Most of the time I was back at my office by 8:30 the following morning.

In 1985 I purchased my first tractor, a 1976 John Deere 4430, at a farm sale. That was an exciting day for me. It was Charlie Eide who built and helped attach a hydraulic lift for this tractor, too.

My 1992 John Deere model 4560 has been
a work horse since I purchased it in 1996.

By 1999 I traded the 4430 for a 1992 John Deere Model 4560 that had front wheel assist. I found the tractor at a dealership in Volga (South Dakota). John Stratmeyer, who worked at the Lennox John Deere dealership for years, was helping me search for this type of tractor. Our hunt led us to the Garretson John Deere dealership, where they told me they might have the tractor I wanted at their Volga dealership.

John and I traveled to Volga and quickly spotted the 4560 on the lot. John still had the universal tractor key he used while working at the dealership. I observed as John hopped into the tractor and started it up. Within seconds a couple of the dealership employees were out on the lot, too. They were probably concerned that someone was attempting to steal a tractor. But we weren't.

After driving the tractor, listening to the engine, and checking it out overall, John gave me a thumbs up on it. He thought it was in good condition. I knew it had features I wanted and would give me the power I needed on the farm. After thinking over the $55,000 sale price for a few days, I struck a deal with the Garretson dealership.

That tractor, which my cousin purchased in 2021, served as my workhorse.

As time went on, I bought other machinery – a field cultivator, disc and whirly mower and a full line of machinery.

As far as I recall, it was 1987 when I rented land from Dad. At first, I rented for a share of the crop. As I developed my own farming routine, Dad and I had different approaches to farming, so it was much simpler for us to do cash rent.

For years Dad's highest corn plant population was probably 18,000 kernels per acre. He thought I was crazy when I increased mine. His opinion began changing as he watched me harvest over 100 bushel-per-acre corn (that was a lot at the time).

In 1992 I purchased an International Hydro Model 70 tractor (my ONLY red tractor) on a neighbor's sale. This tractor had a loader and the kind of slow speed that I wanted when I loaded bales. It also worked well with the bean buggy I bought a few years later. The bean buggy was mounted on the front of the tractor loader so I could adjust the height of the bean buggy riders. Some places the beans were taller, some places they were shorter. This tractor would also just creep through the bean field, which was very convenient if there were a lot of weeds. It gave riders time to thoroughly spray the weeds.

Typically, Mom, Dad, Rita, and Susan Bultena did the spraying while I operated the tractor. At one point I hired some young kids to help, but they had a hard time staying focused on killing weeds, preferring to squirt each other with weed killer. I couldn't allow that.

One thing I miss about using a bean buggy was the opportunity to get an overall view of my field as we worked through it.

Our good friend, Gil Hagenbuch, made a lift for the Hydro and also designed and made many modifications and extensions so I could operate the tractor. He created extensions for many different features on the tractor, and even had an extra mirror on the front that made it possible for me to see behind me.

It was Gil who made the hitching device that allowed me to hitch a flatbed to the tractor without getting off from it. That meant I could hitch, go to the field, load bales, then come back to the farm and unload bales by myself. Hitching was somewhat tricky because I had to get within no less than three inches of the wagon tongue for the hitch to work. Using the rear-view mirror, I was able to get it done.

At that time, Dad hired a farmer with a round baler to put up our hay. For me, it was quite something when I could bring those bales home on my own. The first time I accomplished this, it gave me a great feeling of satisfaction and independence.

When the time came for Dad to retire from the farm, I started renting the farm from them. I hired Richard Poppinga to help me with planting and harvesting. He lived just down the road from us and was always very gracious to help.

Richard was like the energizer bunny, putting in long days planting. I always wanted to stay about two hours ahead of him, which was no easy task. I'd be driving my own tractor, watching Richard and thinking, "Aren't you ever going to get tired and go home so I can go home, too?" A few times I called him on his cell phone.

"Aren't you getting tired?"

"No, was I supposed to?" We loved to tease each other.

After Dad retired from farming, I prepared fields with my field cultivator and roller and Richard Poppinga did all our planting and harvesting.

I'm not sure how Richard got everything done. It's hard to imagine how he found time to sleep! During planting and harvesting, he just didn't quit. Anytime I called him to help me, I'd better be ready for him 15 minutes before he was to come. He was Johnny-On-the-Spot. Anytime I got behind with field preparation, Richard came to help me catch up. If he couldn't help, he sent his hired man.

Richard had a pretty good four-wheel-drive tractor. Any time I got stuck in the field, Richard loved it. He'd bring his red machine to pull my green machine out of the mud. I never had to worry that he'd scold me for getting stuck. He had too much fun pulling me out.

"There's no mud on top of that tractor cab," Richard would tell me. "You weren't stuck too bad." If he didn't spin his wheels while he was pulling me out, that was also a sign that I wasn't stuck very much.

If I did get stuck, I tried to keep from covering the tractor with mud. Rita was the one who had to clean it.

In the first years he helped us, Richard had an eight-row planter and planted 30-inch rows. Eventually he used a 12-row planter, also on 30-inch rows.

When Richard cut back on his farming work, I hired my cousin-in-law, Steve Sinning and his son Alex, who use a 24-row planter on 20-inch rows. Since I'm no longer able to drive a tractor, Rita and I hire them to do all our farming work.

As I think back over the years, I realize that God continually put people in my life that helped make all these things possible. There's no question that so many aspects of my life have been a "God thing."

Among those people who so graciously and competently assisted me in my farming activities was Charles Eide, the first person in our neighborhood who, with no qualms about it, fully accepted me driving tractors. Charlie and Dad worked together for many years at putting up hay and other farm activities. I will always remember the late afternoon that Charlie called me and asked if I would come and rake hay while he milked cows. Generally, there's a small window of time for getting hay baled and under a roof so it doesn't get rained on. Charlie needed a little help to meet his deadlines. I also helped Charlie pick corn. What a thrill it was for me to be asked by someone other than my Dad to come and help out.

As for Gil Hagenbuch, I would have sworn he had gone to engineering school, he was so good at designing modifications for my farming equipment, our Gator, and my gun holder.

I came to know Gil through his son Paul. Gil also bought insurance from me. When I purchased the 4560, you couldn't just move the lift on the 4430 to the new tractor. It had to be custom fitted.

Gil was a perfectionist. The lift had to perfectly fit the 4560. When I went to use it, if it didn't quite work for me, he changed or remade it. He made all kinds of modifications on that tractor and I'll never forget that he understood so well that one inch one way or the other could mean the difference between something working or not working for me.

If I needed to have something modified, I could describe to Gil what I needed. Then he would sit down in his recliner and draw out a design. He told me it sometimes took longer to draw out the design than it did to actually make the piece, especially the intricate extensions he made for my guns. That took some contemplation.

One thing I noticed when I used my 4560 was that, even though I had my seatbelt on, I would continually slide down into the seat and have to push myself back up. It was uncomfortable. I asked Gil if he had any idea about what we could do to remedy that. After giving it some thought, Gil suggested that he make a knee pad for me and position it so that I would only slide down a little bit and no further. His recommendation worked well and made me feel more comfortable when I was running the tractor. The pad could be adjusted so it was as close or as far away as I wanted.

He also added extensions to the tractor's shift lever because shifting into some of the gears pushed the lever too far away for me to reach. He added an extension to the throttle and made a lever I could use to put the power-take-off into and out of gear.

I don't have enough strength in my wrists to start the tractor to or turn it off. To remedy that, Gil made a t-shaped copper device that helped me start the tractor and shut it off. The key was attached to the device and the t-shape allowed me to grasp and use it.

These kinds of small modifications made it possible for me to be as independent as possible. I used that same kind of extension to operate the tractor's heating, cooling, lights, and fan features. Simple devices but so important to me. Gil made sure that I was self-sufficient in the tractor – except when it came to eating.

Gil helped us modify our John Deere Gator so I could operate it. He designed a rod that attached to the throttle that I could use it as a hand throttle. He also extended the shifting handle so I could reach it. To assist Rita in getting me into the Gator seat, Gil modified the seat so it would pivot sideways. Rita could sit me down, then turn the seat back so I was sitting straight. Gil also added an armrest from one of my old wheelchairs to the Gator seat, giving me something to help keep my balance.

We could take the armrest off as I got into the Gator, then put it back on once I was seated. He didn't need to help with a seatbelt. I used a bungee cord for that. But Gil wasn't done. He made a windshield that we could put up or down. And I'm so thankful that he added a horn, too. I love having a horn on everything.

Gil also made a trigger mechanism for all my guns that made it easier for me to pull the trigger. Without the mechanism, my shots would be off because I had to pull the trigger so hard my gun would go sideways. The mechanism was foldable and fit in my gun case.

It was also Gil who designed a device for the door leading to our garage so that, once I'm in the house, I can close the door by myself. With the bar handles on all our doors, I can open them, but I can't reach back to close a door. Gil's pulley system makes it much easier for me to get the door going into the garage closed.

These are all small details of life that most independent people don't even think about. It was sad to watch Gil develop Alzheimer's and eventually pass away. He was a wonderful friend to me and Rita.

The *Farming* FAMILIES
of Turner County
MARCH 2018

Meet
HARLAN
and RITA TEMPLE

FAITH / FAMILY / FRIENDS / FARMING

Photo by AllScapes Photography

We were honored to be featured in this March 2018 Farming Families magazine.

My green line of John Deere tractors include (left to right): 1961 3010 diesel; 1951 Model B; 1949 Model A ; 1960 Model 630.

Niece Shelley and I took a break after giving the Model A a bath.

Of course, when the tractors come out we have to have some fun. Here I'm giving the Model B a pull to get it started!

Harlan Wehde was another great friend. Harlan grew up less than a mile from Rita's family farm. The two of them went to the same country school. Harlan was about five years older than me and remembered seeing me play on the floor with my farm toys at my grandparents' farm when I was a kid.

After I started my insurance business, Harlan had a crop insurance policy with me.

He and his wife Dorothy (both of them now deceased) often came over to play cards with me and Rita. Of course, my hands were stiff enough that I couldn't hold cards. I used a piece of wood that had a cutout at a bit of a slant so I could lean my cards up against it. It didn't work real well. Often my cards fell upside down.

Harlan and I had a lot of fun teaming up against our wives in the card games. If we won, we wrote it down so we would remember who won the next time we played. We never stacked the deck against our wives, but Harlan and I won a lot of those games.

Harlan was a deep thinker and loved to tinker with things. He decided that there must be a better design for a cardholder. He was looking to use pressure so I could tap on a card to push it out when I needed it.

"Sometimes I wake up at night and think about how to draw that out on paper," Harlan told me.

In his quest to improve my cardholder, Harlan came up with three prototypes. He asked me to use each one and see how it worked. "If it doesn't work, I'll go back to the drawing board," he said. With the third prototype, he nailed it.

I am eternally grateful to Harlan Wehde for his diligent work on my card holder. I love playing cards and here I am enjoying a game with USD students Mallary Paitz and Jessica Reishus.

The cardholder he made, which I still use today, holds 12 cards. It also makes it possible for the child in me to occasionally flip a card out of the holder and onto the table. Harlan put the date on the underside of the holder he made and engraved the words, "Made for Harlan Temple by Harlan Wehde (Friends Forever)."

What a blessing to have a friend with such a great desire to help me be as independent as possible! We were able to share Harlan and Dorothy's celebration of their 60th year of farming and 60th wedding anniversary all at the same time.

It really touches my heart when I think of all the people who have given of their time and talents to help me achieve my dreams. If there's one thing I've learned throughout my life it's to know that so many things we want to do can be done. We can never give up. We should always do what we know to be right to help others. Never live just for yourself. Help others live life to the very fullest as much as God enables us. That's what brings lasting happiness.

My cousins (left to right): Standing - Cinda, Peggy, Pam, Joanie, Sharon, me, and Jeannie. The little girl on the right is Sarah.

136

Pictured above, at Mom and Dad's 40th wedding anniversary on October 8, 1980, are Mom's sisters Jeanette and Pearl, Mom, and her brother George. Pictured below are Dad with his sisters Ida (left) and Angie.

*"Be devoted to
one another in love.
Honor one another
above yourselves."*

ROMANS 12:10

NINE

FAMILY TIES

For my Dad, family was at the heart of his life. He was born September 22, 1916, on a farm just three-fourths of a mile from where we now live. As I sit in our sun-room, I can look across the landscape and see the trees still standing on that farm.

Since Dad struggled to fit into the blended family after his mother remarried, he rotated between the homes of aunts and uncles until Lena and George Symens all but adopted him. He stayed with them most of the time until he was about 15.

Over the years, I recall Dad and his stepfather, Enno Stratmeyer, playing horseshoes when we had summer gatherings. I always remember that Enno was kind to me.

We called Dad's mother, Oma, too. She and Enno lived in a large, six-bedroom house. A staircase in the middle of the house led up to the second story. After Enno passed away, Ardie and I stayed overnight sometimes for a multi-day "vacation" with Oma. To us kids, the house seemed like a hotel. Upstairs was a large bathtub that was fun to bathe in. We could choose the room we wanted to sleep in. One bedroom was known as Aunt Ida's room. It was where she slept as she grew up. Another room was referred to as Aunt Angie's room. In the morning, Oma always made a big breakfast for us.

Mere words will never convey all the ways my parents and sisters have blessed me since the day I was born. I know my parents put their faith and trust in God. We never talked about it, but they must have taken God's instructions to heart when they read and studied scriptures such as Joshua 1:9. "Have I not commanded you? Be strong and courageous. Do not be afraid; do not be discouraged, for the LORD your God will be with you wherever you go."

As a child, there was never a time that I sensed I was a burden or in any way a disappointment to my parents. I attribute much of this to the fact that Mom and Dad were dedicated to regularly attending church and practicing the godly principles they learned there. The best gift they could ever have given us was to teach us about Jesus and the salvation we find in Him. From the first day of our life, we had this valuable foundation to build upon.

My mother was small in stature, but her physical energy and enthusiasm for life were monumental. I will never forget her scurrying about the house, the farmyard, and her garden, often staying active from dawn till dark as she cared for her family and helped Dad with chores.

Dad was reasonably quiet and a very patient and kind person. Even though I was somewhat closer to Mom than to Dad, whenever we kids wanted something, we went to Dad. Mom was more protective of her children, more on the strict side with us, and less willing to allow us to take the risks that so often captured my attention! And it's common for a mother to be more protective of her children.

I'm deeply grateful that Dad was willing to let me live my life, seek and explore new experiences. However, when it came to talking about internal thoughts and feelings, Mom was more willing to share at a deeper level. Dad would talk about experiences he had as a child or a young man, but his conversations seldom led to deep discussions.

Both my parents were hard-working people who gave their all to whatever task they accomplished. Both grew up on the farm and learned how to work and enjoy the simple things in life.

From what Dad told me, he struck out on his own when he was about 15, living pretty independently and making his own living. Dad worked for farmers to earn an income. One of those farmers was Henry and Clara Sinning, a relative of a cousin's spouse. Down the road, the Sinning's grandson Steve married my cousin Patty.

John DeVries was another farmer who employed my Dad at one time. Years later, in 1960, their son, Ervin, married my sister Ardie. Life brings so many intriguing connections.

As I noted in an earlier chapter, we were so blessed with a harmonious home. My parents loved each other deeply and weren't afraid to show their affection for one another.

Ardie not only gave of her time to help with my daily care, but she also pitched in with all the daily housekeeping chores: washing dishes, laundry, vacuuming, etc. There were probably times when she thought that I was the family brat. It was true I was more of a mamma's boy, and she was undoubtedly daddy's girl. Even though we kids gravitated toward one parent or the other, we felt equally loved by both Mom and Dad.

Of course, we had our moments of sibling rivalry. I was sometimes jealous that Ardie was able to drive the tractor for events like threshing. That was something I didn't get to do. Still, from little on, Ardie and I were and still are very close to one another.

Once in a great while Ardie drove me back to CCHS. After graduating from high school and taking a job in Sioux Falls at a gas company, she sometimes came over to CCHS to visit me.

I don't remember this incident, but Ardie tells me she once walked to CCHS at the end of her workday, then walked back home. That trek would have spanned at least a couple of miles each way. I take this as another indication of Ardie's devotion to her brother. I recall one other occasion when Ardie's boyfriend picked me up and drove me to Ardie's apartment (which she shared with two other girls). That was an excellent opportunity for me to see Ardie and sneak in a smoke and have a break from CCHS.

When she married and moved 750 miles away (to Holland, Michigan), my family I struggled to see them move that far away. Her husband, Ervin, first worked at the Buick garage in Cherokee, Iowa, for one year in an apprenticeship program. In August of 1963 they moved to Springfield, South Dakota, where Ervin attended Southern State College. In the fall of 1965, they moved to Yankton, South Dakota, where he did his internship at the Chevrolet garage while Ardie worked at Gurney Seed Company. In 1966 they moved to Holland, Michigan, where Ervin took a job at Ottawa County District School as an auto mechanic teacher. Ardie worked as a secretary at the Ottawa County high school business office.

Kevin and Shelley, Ardie's and Ervin's children, were both born in Iowa. Robert and Deborah were both born in Michigan.

Despite the miles that have separated us for so many years, we have always called and written to each other frequently and remained in close touch. I love to tease Ardie and tell her it's a brother's obligation to do so. I often tell her a story she isn't sure she ought to believe, but we have a deep respect for one another. I'm blessed with this neat person as my sister.

One year, at Christmas, Mom and Dad and I were planning a trip to Michigan to see Ardie and her family. Initially, we planned to start out early in the morning. But I was a night owl. I was convinced We could drive all night and have some extra time to spend at Ardie's.

It was 10:30 or even later that evening when we got on the road. By the time we were just south of Beresford, I noticed there wasn't much traffic. The traffic we did see was moving pretty slowly. I'd better test the road.

Sure enough, the road was icy. At that point we probably should have just turned around and gone back home. However, optimists that we are, we believed road conditions would probably get better the further we went. As we traveled on, we found that the opposite was true. By the time we reached I-80 near Council Bluffs, Iowa, the roads were terrible. I could drive 25 to 30 miles per hour at best. So many people had gone in the ditch or gotten hung up on the highway meridian and left their flashing lights on that the interstate looked like a Christmas tree.

Before too long we came upon another vehicle and saw that someone needed help. When Dad stepped out of our vehicle, he nearly fell. The road was super slick. We told the stranded motorist we would stop at the next gas station we came to and send back help.

When we reached that gas station, they had already been flooded with requests for help. We were determined to continue driving. Maybe we would drive out of it soon.

At one point, I nearly went into the ditch. I know God grabbed the wheel and kept us on the road. We came to a full stop, then started out again. We came upon a snowplow that had a train of cars following behind. At least he was pushing the snow off the road, but it was still dangerously icy.

One thing that may have helped us on that trip was the new studded tires I had just put on my 1967 Pontiac. We also had the car loaded with meat and Christmas gifts. The trunk was definitely carrying a lot of weight.

We crept along, finally getting past Des Moines and close to the Illinois border. Dad had mentioned that, whenever I was ready, he could take over driving. We were a short way inside the Illinois line when I told Dad I couldn't drive any further. He would have to take the wheel. I had been straining so hard to see the road my eyes were bugging out of my head.

Once Dad got behind the wheel, I immediately fell asleep. And wouldn't you know, about 15 miles down the road we hit dry pavement! Dad drove across the Indiana border, then I got behind the wheel again, just before we drove into more snow!

It should have taken us about 11.5 hours to drive to Ardie's house. Instead, it took 18.5 hours. It was getting dark again by the time we arrived there. Erv and Ardie had been watching the weather reports so they knew we were coming across some bad roads. At that time, with no cell phones, just pay phones along the way, we would have only delayed our travel time by stopping to call them. When we stopped for gas, we didn't think about giving them a call. We were focused on making it to Holland, Michigan.

It was interesting that word had spread to Erv and Ardie's whole neighborhood about our treacherous trip, and they had all been praying for us. When we drove into Erv and Ardie's driveway, everyone up and down street came out to wave and express their thanks that we were safe and sound. It was like a great big welcoming party.

We were also thanking God for safe passage. We had not only seen cars and semi-trucks in the ditch, some buses couldn't stay on the road either. None of us had verbalized it, but there moments when we wondered why we were still out there.

My parents told Ardie and Erv that we would think twice before coming to Michigan at Christmas time again. My parents did make more trips, and eventually flew there for the holiday.

There was no doubt that God had traveled with us that night.

After that year, we went to see Ardie and Erv in the summer. Erv had built a cabin cruiser that was between 30 and 34 feet long. He made it out of a kit. On our visits we took the cruiser out on Lake Michigan to fish. Rita went with us one time, but she got so seasick she never went out again. While the boat was moving she seemed to be okay. But when we stopped to fish the movement of the boat didn't set well with her. We had to go back to shore.

Jim and Max Brown and their family were neighbors to Ardie and Erv. When we went to visit, all of us were like one big happy family. Ardie and Erv's house was right by Lake Macatawa. The channel of this lake leads into Lake Michigan. There was just a street between them and the water. The Brown's home was right on the water, and they had a boat dock we often used.

Jim also had a cabin cruiser and took us out on the lake sometimes. I recall that Jim never got in a hurry about anything. If he said he wanted to go somewhere about four o'clock, it would probably be closer to five before we got going. Jim would find one more thing he needed to do.

On one visit, Dad and Erv were out fishing and got caught in a storm. They were able to get the boat to a bay in another nearby

144

town. It was so late in the day that they called us to tell us where they were, then spent the night on the boat. Because of the storm, they were nearly 25 miles away from home but they made it home the following day.

In later years, Rita and I once stayed with Max Brown; Jim had passed away. We came to Michigan for Deborah's wedding and Ardie and Erv's house was already full of guests. Max spoiled us rotten, making breakfast and serving us as if we were staying in a hotel.

When Jim was alive, he and Max brought their camper to our farm every year. They parked on the folks' yard and were content to spend their time here just sitting on the yard and enjoying the quiet country life and wide open spaces.

"It's so relaxing to be in the country and watch the sunset," they told us. We coaxed them into doing some sightseeing, but not much.

One summer their son Mike and Ardie's son Kevin decided to sleep in a tent on the lawn. During the night a thunderstorm blew in and quickly blew the tent down. The boys dashed into the house, and slept inside for the remainder of their visit.

Since they were staying in a camper, Jim and Max used our outdoor privy during their visits. At the time we had a Blue Heeler named Chico. This breed of dogs is very protective of their owners.

Halfway through the night Jim got up to go to the outhouse. Halfway back to the camper, Chico met him and wasn't about to allow him to go any further.

Jim wasn't certain how to proceed and couldn't for the life of him remember Chico's name. He called out every name he could think of, then finally remembered, Chico! As soon as he heard his name, the dog decided Jim was probably okay and allowed him to return to the camper.

It was funny to hear Jim telling the story, but it probably wasn't so funny for him to be cornered by the dog in the middle of the night.

Jim and Max's kids, Kathy and Chrissie, always enjoyed gathering eggs with Mom when they visited us. We took turns having supper at Mom and Dad's and at our house. It was just a few years after Rita and I married that Jim passed away. We continued to stay in touch with Max until she passed. Now we stay connected to their kids. It was somewhat difficult for Ardie to sell their home after Erv passed away. He had done a lot of work to make the home a very nice place to live. It held many fond memories. A friend, who was a teacher, had given Erv a lot of help with the work.

I'll always remember the time Henry, and his new bride Jean came to our farm on their honeymoon. They were friends of Ardie and Ervin. They ended up sleeping in the same room I was in. We always teased them about how much fun it was to spend your honeymoon with someone else in the room. They didn't seem to care.

I found it interesting too that, while they were here, we had a rain shower, and Henry went outside and took a shower in the rain.

Chrissie and her husband Jim came to visit us several years ago. She is crazy as a hoot, like me and my niece, Shelley. She's full of life and I hope she never changes. While she was here we never had a dull moment.

Whenever Ardie and her family visit us, they're always helping us out. Robert isn't always able to come along, but when he does he's more than willing to help. When he's here, Robert always cleans my guns, which is much appreciated. One year they asked if we would care if they put LED lights in our garage because it was on the dark side. We were fine with that, and Kevin and his sisters went ahead and bought everything we needed to get the job done. When they finished that project, they went to the machine shed and put LED lights there, too. They've helped with trimming trees and Kevin even set up a weather station for me.

Afterward, we took all the John Deere's out of the shed and gave them a bath. It's common for Kevin and his siblings to mow the lawn while they're here, too. When we used to mow the lawn together (I can't do it anymore, too hard on my back), we finished up with lawn mower races. Deborah, Ardie's youngest daughter, brought her significant other with her a few times. He was very adept at repairing and fixing our John Deere's and adjusting some things so the tractors ran better.

It's so rewarding to have loving family who do their best to help out in such practical ways. We never tire of having them visit and enjoying their company. The time always goes too fast while they're here.

I have always been close to Ardie's family. One year, when I had one of my John Deere tractors in the Lennox parade, Shelley and Deborah rode with me and threw candy out to the kids who were among the crowd that lined the streets.

On April 14, 1954, we welcomed my sister Joan into the world. Even though the three of us had our moments of sibling rivalry, we were always close. As she grew up, Joanie sometimes got into Ardie's things, but Ardie was well aware of how much Joanie looked up to her big sister.

Joanie, who had Down Syndrome, brought many unique blessings to our family. While Down Syndrome is characterized by some physical attributes such as a short neck, flattened facial profile and nose, and upward slanting eyes, Down Syndrome also causes delayed physical development that affects sitting and walking, learning disabilities, and cognitive impairment. In a farming household where one child already required a great deal of physical care, Joan's birth must have often kept Mom on her knees, seeking strength and direction from God. However, as I already mentioned, there was never a time any of us kids experienced anything but our parents' deepest love and most generous care.

Just as Mom and Dad had done with me as a child, they treated Joanie like any other child. She was able to go to school, and she had chores every day like Ardie and me.

For some reason, Joanie rarely called me Harlan. She usually referred to me as "Brother."

Joanie lived at home with my parents for most of her life. In 2004, when Mom developed a life-threatening bowel obstruction that led to major surgery and the need for nursing home care, Dad took care of Joanie for a time.

Then, in March 2005, Joanie caught her foot in the corner of her bedspread and, in some odd, twisting fall, broke her femur. Dad would not be able to take care of her while she recuperated. She spent three days in the hospital, then she also needed nursing home care to recover. Joanie went to the same home in Lennox where Mom was staying.

With Mom at her side, Joanie was quite comfortable at the nursing home. Her leg healed enough that she could forego a wheelchair. Even though Joanie and Mom had separate rooms at the nursing home, Mom led Joanie in devotions every night before they went to bed. She often helped residents back and forth to the dining room, an activity she immensely enjoyed. And Joanie and Mom spent a lot of time together.

Eventually, some policy changes made by the State required that Joanie be moved to a different facility. According to the policy, having Joanie as a resident was "housing the mentally handicapped," a function outside the scope of the nursing home mission. Joanie and Mom weren't the only ones disappointed with the change. The nursing home staff loved Joanie and enjoyed having her there.

Joanie never did understand why, suddenly, she had to leave Mom and her friends at the nursing home. The experience was heartbreaking for all of us. Dad still lived at home, but he wasn't able to care for her.

Joanie sat on her bed, knowing that this was the day she would have to move.

"Brother!" she sobbed. "Don't let them take me!"

Joanie's tears and her fearful, despairing state brought back very negative memories of my own days at CCHS. I hated being away from my family and feeling as if I was in prison. My own heart anguished over the knowledge that I couldn't do anything to help her except be there, supporting her as much as possible.

"We don't have anything to say about it, Joanie." I repeated those words over and over. But her broken heart just couldn't understand. I felt that, in some way, I was receiving pay back for all my rebellious defiance during those first years at CCHS.

When Joanie moved to Lifescape, she was doing well physically. She didn't require any assistance with walking, but she needed a lot of attention to navigate everyday life. At the time, Dad's health was declining, and it was out of the question for him to take on caring for her. Rita already had her hands full with Dad along with the care I required, so we had no other options.

I told myself that, just as I had learned how to get through my time at the school, Joanie would come to accept the change. But she never did accept her move to a group home.

The first while that Joanie was at Lifescape, we brought her home on weekends to enjoy time with family. Often, either our friends Marlin and Susan Bultena or Joyce Stratmeyer picked Joanie up at Lifescape and brought her to the nursing home where Mom lived. That way Dad could pick Joanie up and bring her home. Every Sunday night, when it was time for her to return to Lifescape, Joanie cried and carried on, not wanting to return. Her behavior and emotional distress brought on powerful flashbacks from my own nightmare of separating from family to return to CCHS. Joanie cried and carried on almost every Sunday night.

When she lived in a group home setting at Lifescape, Joanie went to the main building every day to work on crafts, puzzles, and jewelry making. Joanie made some beautiful jewelry.

Eventually, Lifescape opened a specific site where residents worked at jewelry making. Because of Joanie's overall joyful approach to life, in the five years she lived at Lifescape she captured the hearts of many Lifescape staff members. Some of the staff who cared for her became lifelong friends of our entire family.

One of Joanie's doctors told us that, at some point, most Down Syndrome individuals develop Alzheimer's. It's not a matter of if, but a matter of when. It's part of their genetic makeup. Just as predicted, we saw this disease start taking over Joanie during the last three years of her life. Her physical stamina quickly declined to the point where she wasn't able to walk without a walker. Before long, she didn't want to try and walk anymore, which led to the use of a wheelchair. Soon, Joanie lost interest in eating and drinking. This stage quickly led to dehydration. By this time, Joanie was in need of hospice care.

Joanie's hospice nurse called me on a Thursday morning, asking if we wanted to let Joanie go to Jesus or have her transported to the hospital. Did we want to take measures to prolong her life?

Mom, Dad, and I had talked over and agreed upon how we would handle things if it came to this point.

"We don't want to prolong Joanie's suffering," I told the nurse. "She just needs to go to Jesus."

The day after that conversation, I received another call. Joanie was failing quickly, more quickly than expected. It was paramount that all of us gather around her as soon as possible because she was definitely in the final moments of her life journey.

Ardie had planned to come to see all of us the following week, but her son's wife, Jill, told Kevin, "You need to take your mother now." Ardie and Kevin quickly packed what they needed and got on the road early Friday morning and reached the farm that evening.

At this time, on June 18, 2011, both Mom and Dad were in the nursing home, sharing the same room. I wanted some time alone with Joanie, so I went ahead while Rita picked up Mom and Dad and brought them to Lifescape. We gave them some time alone with Joanie. That same morning, our Pastor Harlan and his wife Verlainne came. Later two cousins, Patty and Brenda, and my Aunt Ida also came.

Throughout the day, we all held vigil, going back and forth, taking turns at Joanie's bedside. Different Lifescape staff members stopped in Joanie's room to say their goodbyes. Several of the workers came even though it was a day off. Two of them were young women who were spending the day at a nearby water park. When they received the email that said Joanie was soon to pass away, they wanted the opportunity to tell her goodbye.

All of us were by Joanie's side as she lived out those final few hours of her life. Even though she had become difficult to manage as Alzheimer's took over her mind, Joanie was loved by so many people outside our family circle. The gals who left the water park to see her gave her a final tender hug. Her room was filled with so many loving, caring people.

"It's okay, Joanie," Mom whispered. "Just go to Jesus." Mom held one of Joanie's hands, and Aunt Ida held the other. After about an hour, Joanie took a deep breath, then paused. Another deep breath, a pause, and then the third and final breath. Her entire body relaxed, and we knew she was now in her heavenly home with Jesus.

The hospice chaplain shared scripture and led all of us in prayer as we took up the vigil beside Joanie.

It was a bittersweet and sacred moment to see Joanie go. However, knowing she was released from the limitations she had known all her life was comforting. One of the hospice nurses who was there with us suggested we sing a familiar doxology. We all sang together. It was a very touching experience. Death can be a beautiful thing when we know we're going home to be with the Lord. I don't have a death wish. But, in what I know are my final years, I'm often homesick.

"Would you like to hold her for a few minutes?" A nurse posed the question to Mom, who was seated in a wheelchair.

Mom answered, "Yes. I would like to hold her one more time."

It was a great blessing for Mom to hold Joanie now because Joanie hadn't wanted anything to do with cuddling in the last year of her life. Every time Joanie pulled away from her (we never knew what brought on this behavior), we could see that this hurt Mom. So, holding her for even a few moments helped ease the pain of Mom's loss. I regret not doing the same. It was a missed opportunity.

Afterward, the Group Home's lead person insisted that she would bathe Joanie for the last time. It seemed that gave her closure after caring for Joanie for three years. She was at different group home for the previous two years.

We will always know that Joanie touched many more lives than we can imagine. One of the most extraordinary things we all learned from Joanie was unconditional love and patience. I remember so well her standard comment when we asked her if she had finished a chore, such as cleaning her room.

"I'm going to," she would tell us.

One time, after Rita and I were married, Joan clashed with Rita over something Joan was supposed to do. Joan didn't hesitate to express her displeasure at being pressured to follow through.

"Why did you marry her?" she asked me. We still chuckle about that.

At our house, Joanie's birthday, April 14, was always treated like a national holiday. She loved celebrating her birthday and would begin talking about the day months ahead of time. One year, at the nursing home, we had family and numerous guests helping her celebrate the occasion.

Joanie wasn't doing the best on that birthday. Instead of her usual sunny disposition, she slipped into an anxiety attack. Soon, Dad's eyes welled up with tears. He always considered Joanie to be his baby. We knew we had to get her back to Mom's room and help her calm down, or the joy of the day would be lost. Kali and I took Joanie to Mom's room, where we had a prayer and a talk with her. Thankfully, we were able to help Joanie regain her composure, and we all enjoyed the rest of the evening.

The last year Joanie was alive, her birthday fell on a weekday. We talked to the Lifescape aide, Kali, who generally brought Joanie to the nursing home, where we all gathered around Mom for Sunday afternoon visits. Our thought was that we should celebrate Joanie's birthday over the weekend. This would save the aide an extra trip.

"No, Harlan," Kali said. "I sense that we need to celebrate her birthday on the day. I feel it in my heart. This will be Joanie's last birthday on earth."

I'm glad we listened to Joanie's loving caretaker. I don't know how she knew, but Kali was absolutely correct as Joanie passed away in June of that year. It seems some people have the gift of a sixth sense.

I have so many precious memories of my beloved mother. Besides working diligently alongside Dad to help with milking chores and doing chicken chores, Mom cooked, baked, kept a cozy, inviting home, and lavished us kids with all the love in her heart.

Though Mom's life was very busy with her children and providing all the extra care Joanie and I needed, she was also very active at church. I think she took part in nearly every program the church had going.

One of my fond memories of Mom is the trips she made to the field to bring me and Dad lunch in the morning and the afternoon. I'll never forget the hot egg sandwiches she made during corn harvest. She delivered the sandwiches in a baggy to help keep them hot. It was often 9:30 in the forenoon when she came to the field, our dog Chico at her side. As I ate my sandwich, the dog sat next to the tractor, gazing longingly at my snack. I always had to save a bite for Chico. He loved the sandwiches as much as I did!

In some weird kind of accident, Mom fell in the garage and broke her arm and wrist. Of course, that meant surgery, which she came through just fine. However, when she developed a bowel obstruction, Mom was so ill before the major surgery she needed, we weren't sure she would survive. Spunky Mom! She was hospitalized for several days after this second surgery, but God spared her life. When she was released from the hospital, the doctor ordered nursing home care for approximately one week before Mom could return home.

That same week, Rita and I had planned to travel to Pierre (South Dakota) for the annual deer hunting event we had participated in for several years. As we visited Mom before leaving on our trip, she was already walking with a walker and appeared to be recovering nicely.

Rita and I were gone for three days. We couldn't have imagined how we found Mom when we returned.

We never did find out what happened to Mom in those three

days that we were gone, but she couldn't walk when we went to see her. Her back was hurting her, and the nursing home staff told us she would not be able to go home as we had planned. She would have to be mobile before she could be dismissed.

We were dumbfounded and so disheartened. The situation didn't seem right, but no one appeared to know for sure what had caused Mom to regress. Not only was Mom a great blessing to us kids and her family, throughout her life, she also touched the lives of so many people. Always so full of life, Mom gardened, baked, worked with so many chores, and was very active in the church. Her life circumstances seemed so unfair.

For three more years, Mom resided at the nursing home. While her recovery had taken much longer than expected, she was now doing well, and it appeared that she would finally be able to return to the farm.

Shortly before she was due to be released from the nursing home, Mom was rocking in her gliding rocker. She decided to sit in a different chair that was nearby. When she reached across the rocking chair to grasp the other chair, the rocker she was in tipped over. Mom fell to the floor, which caused her to break her shoulder.

This happened about 10:30 in the evening. Mom was so disappointed and unhappy with herself. Rita and I spent the night with her in the hospital. Needless to say, after that incident, Mom never had another opportunity to go home.

Of course, this was all very difficult for Dad. He and Mom had been inseparable all the years of their marriage. Now they were forced to live apart. Of course, Dad did everything he could to be with her throughout that time. He visited her every day. I don't believe Dad ever missed one. Every day, right after lunch, he went to the nursing home and spent the afternoon with Mom. They ate supper together at the nursing home, then Dad would go home for the night.

On Sundays, we sometimes brought Mom home for a meal. There was never a time when she was truly ready to return to the nursing home.

One evening, it was raining hard, the wind was blowing. Weather-wise, it was a very unpleasant evening. For the entire time that Mom was in the nursing home, Dad's habit was to call her once he was back home. That night, nearly one hour after he headed home, Mom hadn't received his call. She called me.

"You need to check on your dad," she said. "I'm worried about him."

Rita and I lived one-fourth mile from Mom and Dad's house. We could look across the field and see if there was a light in the house. Dad constantly left a little light on at night. Rita hurriedly looked toward their house. There was no light.

"I'll go over and check on him," Rita said. She jumped in our vehicle and quickly drove to their house. Dad's car was not in the garage.

We called nearby friends and neighbors, asking if they had seen anything of Dad. Then we called the Sheriff's office to alert them of his disappearance.

Our neighbors, Joan Muller and her husband Glenn, knew Dad well. About 90 minutes after we had alerted people in the neighborhood, Joan called us to say she had found Dad on a nearby road. We were so relieved to know she found him. It was terrifying to not know where he might have been, especially when the weather was so ugly.

"He's very distraught but otherwise okay," she told us. "I offered to drive him the rest of the way home, so he's home now."

Sadly, that was the first episode that led to Dad's diagnosis of dementia and his admission to the nursing home.

It was comforting to my family and me to see Mom and Dad together in the nursing home. It was such a blessing that they were allowed to share in the same room. Even though Dad continued to lose cognizance of his surroundings and physical capabilities, he always remembered to tell Mom one thing: I love you.

Dad must have repeated those words to her 50 times a day. Once in a while, you could see that his constant repetition of the phrase agitated her, but she never let him know it. Any time Dad was near Mom, he held her hand. The love they had shared from the beginning never diminished. They remained close right to the end of Dad's life.

As long as Mom and Dad were alive, we did our best to bring them to the farm for frequent visits. Poor Dad. So often, he was afraid that if the two of them didn't get back to the nursing home before dark, they wouldn't be able to get in. Mom was always ready to linger with us, but we often gave into Dad's concerns and took them back before Mom was really ready.

After he was in the nursing home for some time, Dad began complaining of pain in his stomach. All his life, Dad had been one to endure significant pain. I recall one incident when he was greasing our corn picker. His pinky was caught up in the picker's chain and quickly severed. Dad was done picking that day, but the next day, with his bandaged hand, Dad and I were back in the field.

I've always thought God provided special protection that year. I picked 99 loads of corn and never had one single breakdown. Generally a gathering chain slips off or something goes awry. It seemed to me that an uneventful corn picking experience was a God-given gift because I couldn't have fixed equipment. With his bandaged hand, Dad would have struggled to get something fixed. Whatever the case, having the picker perform so well was a great blessing that year.

But now, the pain in Dad's stomach seemed unbearable. He sometimes screamed and yelled from the discomfort. That wasn't at all like him. Despite all the x-rays and testing, doctors were unable to determine what might be causing the pain. From that point, Dad continued to decline physically and mentally as time went on.

The last time I saw Dad, it was Memorial Day weekend. Rita and I were on our way home from Sioux Falls, and it was late in the evening, probably about 10:30. When we stopped at the nursing home that night, Rita stayed in the van while I dashed in to see Dad. When I reached his bedside, he was asleep. We knew that Dad was failing, and his days were now numbered. In conversations with

156

Dad's nurse, we knew that he would likely go to his heavenly home before long. However, it appeared that it would be a few more days before that moment arrived.

I woke him for just a few minutes.

"Dad, Rita, and I will be in Nebraska tomorrow to visit Mervin's grave and his family, so we won't stop in to see you tomorrow. But we'll be back to see you the day after tomorrow." Whether Dad understood me or not, he nodded his head. I patted his hand, told him I loved him, and allowed him to go back to sleep. Before leaving, I chatted with his nurse again. I wanted to be sure that Dad would be okay until we got back.

"We expect his passing will be within the next three days or so," the nurse said.

The next morning Rita and I set out on our trip. After visiting Mervin's grave, we drove over to see his family. We had just gotten out of the van in their yard and started looking over some landscaping they had recently done when my phone rang.

"Harlan?" It was Dad's nurse. "I just wanted to call and tell you that your father just passed away." I gripped the phone in stunned silence, absolutely shocked by his words. Dad had passed on, and I wasn't there to be with him. I was heartbroken at losing him and deeply saddened about missing those last moments of his life.

Rita and I quickly got back into the van and headed north. I was so concerned about Mom being by herself. I called Joel Klusmann, the mortician who had been a longtime friend and an attendant at our wedding.

"Joel, Rita and I are on our way home from Nebraska, and we got the call that Dad passed away. Can you go to the nursing home and stay with Mom until one of our cousins or my aunt gets there? We'll get there as quickly as we can, but we're at least two hours away, and I don't want Mom to have to face this all by herself."

Joel didn't hesitate to say yes as he was already with her. He remained with Mom until family members arrived. He wouldn't allow Mom to be by herself.

We learned later that Dad had probably passed away an hour or two before the nursing home staff realized it. He hadn't gone to dinner in the dining room, but no one checked on him right then. Mom would later say that, possibly, Dad had quietly passed while she was in the room with him, and she didn't realize it.

Dad was 96 when he died. He and Mom had been married nearly 73 years.

"I would have loved to have him with me just a little longer," Mom said. "I wasn't ready to let him go yet."

We knew that, with his passing, Dad was released from the pain he had experienced with advancing age. We were thankful for that blessing. Still, the separation death brings is painful.

Mom was also 96 when she passed away two years later.

That weekend, my sister Ardie and her son Kevin came for the weekend, intending to visit Mom. Since Mom and Dad had been in the nursing home, our tradition had been to bring her to the farm for a day, usually Sunday, for dinner. Those times we shared quickly became treasured memories.

When Ardie and Kevin went to the nursing home on Saturday morning, they intended to bring Mom out to the farm for the day. However, Mom wasn't feeling well. She was disappointed and unhappy with herself that she didn't feel up to the visit.

Ardie and Kevin planned to stay until Monday, so they went to see Mom again on Sunday. She still wasn't doing well, so they weren't able to bring her to the farm. Because they hadn't been able to visit with Mom as they hoped, at Sunday evening's supper Kevin suggested they stay one more day in hopes that Mom would feel better by Monday. Another God thing.

Monday, right after lunch, Ardie and Kevin went to the nursing home. Mom seemed so much better. She was chatty, perky, and feeling well. The three of them had an enjoyable visit.

Rita had supper ready when Ardie and Kevin returned to the farm. They were thankful they had stayed to share that time with Mom. We had just finished supper when the phone rang. It was the nursing home.

"Harlan? You may want to come to the nursing home right

away. We believe your mother is dying."

I looked around at Rita, Ardie, and Kevin. We couldn't believe what we heard. It had been only an hour since Ardie and Kevin had seen Mom so perky and well.

Kevin stayed behind to clear the supper table while Ardie, Rita, and I rushed to the nursing home. We were halfway to Lennox when the head nurse called said, "No need to rush. Your mother has passed."

When we arrived at her room, Mom was lying on her bed, looking as though she was simply sleeping. We had some time to say "Goodbye for now. You're free, Mom."

The head nurse explained to us that, after Ardie and Kevin left, Mom had asked the nurse's aide if she could have a bowl of soup. Of course, the aide brought the soup, and Mom ate it. Then Mom asked the aide if she could leave the room for a bit.

The nurse's aide, new on the job, wanted to check with the Head Nurse before agreeing to Mom's request. The Head Nurse said Mom could certainly leave her room if she wanted to.

Once the aide returned to Mom's room to give the okay, she noticed that Mom was breathing rather heavily. The nurse aide summoned help quickly, and the Head Nurse responded to her call.

"I held one of your mother's hands, and the nurse aide held the other," the Head Nurse explained. "We told Sophie it was okay; she should just go to Jesus."

With those words, Mom had bowed her head and passed on to her heavenly home.

Talk about a beautiful, peaceful passing. We were so thankful the nurses witnessed Mom's last moments and shared that with us. Just knowing how things had gone made it easier for me to accept her death. Without their report, I would have always wondered about Mom's last minutes on earth.

As much as all of us would have preferred to be with Mom as she passed away, it was very comforting to know the nurses had encouraged her to go to Jesus. We all knew that having missed

Dad since his passing, and at the age of 96, Mom was more than ready for her heavenly home.

Our close friend, Joyce Stratmeyer, also added insight into Mom's final hours before her death. Joyce visited Mom often in those final weeks of Mom's life. Typically, Mom always requested that Joyce "stay a bit longer," not wanting the visit to end. But that day, the day Mom passed away, she didn't ask Joyce to remain and said, "Goodbye, Joyce," as Joyce moved toward the door of Mom's room.

"She never said goodbye when I visited," Joyce told us. We all knew Mom didn't like goodbyes.

"Her words immediately struck me," Joyce said. "I turned to her and said, 'Sophie! We never say goodbye. We always say see you later.'"

Mom didn't respond to Joyce's words. She just smiled.

"At the time, I thought her comment seemed odd," Joyce said. "But I didn't realize I would never see her again. It's almost as if she knew it was her time."

I strongly feel that Mom knew that day she would be heading for heaven very quickly.

It was such a blessing that Mom was very alert and aware of her surroundings, right till her last moments. I'll always wonder if she did know how close her last hours were. When we're reunited in heaven, I may have to ask her, "Why didn't you tell us?"

As with Joanie and Dad, we knew Mom had touched many lives over the years. Altogether, she spent nine years in the nursing home. Though our hearts ached with the separation, Mom's passing also brought joy because we knew she was at peace and with the Lord.

John and Joyce Stratmeyer are Dad's distant relatives and have been very good friends to our family. We called them our "Minutemen" because it seemed no matter when we called, they were able to help us meet a need in no time.

I called John if I needed help with an old tractor that wouldn't start or needed repair. John worked at a John Deere dealership for many years and was well acquainted with how our two-cylinder John Deere tractors worked. I still rely on him to help with my vintage John Deere tractors.

Joyce is a great seamstress. All I had to do was mention the fact that I was in need of a bib, and here she comes with not just one but three bibs, all featuring my favorite logo: John Deere. As long as I've known her, if I mentioned something I needed, I had it.

Joyce was a wonderful help when Mom and Dad and Joanie were in the hospital. Joyce was always ready to sit with them, spend the night, or whatever was required.

It's a blessing to know people who are so willing and ready to lend a hand.

Before children with physical limitations were fully integrated into the public school system, Joyce operated a Day Center where people with disabilities could spend the day working with crafts like making rugs, jewelry, woodworking, etc. Joyce taught young children and provided cooking and baking lessons for those who were able and willing to learn.

A couple of high school students came after school to help Day Center participants with skills such as math and penmanship.

A Day Center activity we so appreciated when Joanie went there was the Thursday afternoon Bible teaching, a Sunday School of sorts. Joyce taught participants scripture and presented biblical lessons each week. Even though most of the attendants took part in similar activities in their own homes, Joyce believed it was important for them to experience biblical teaching. We always saw it as a wonderful gift for these precious people.

In the summer of 2020, Joy (George and Lena's daughter) and her daughter-in-law, Patty and granddaughter Ann visited us. For many years Joy lived in Cambridge, Minnesota, on a farm she and her husband and five sons had acquired. After Joy sold her farm, she and two sons were still living in Minnesota. Another lived in Washington State and one had moved to Montana. After the sale of the farm, Joy decided to join her son and his family in Montana. She was 92 at the time and we couldn't believe how adventurous she was to make that move at an advanced age. Now she and her two sons live near Corvallis, Montana.

The Saturday that they arrived at our home, Joy's family came in a motor home which they parked on our yard. Patty and Ann are walkers and bikers. They both rode their bicycles for a few miles that same evening. I followed them with my wheelchair.

On Sunday we invited other family members for an afternoon lunch. That day, Ann discussed with us the road information she had downloaded from the Internet. Who knew you could do that?

Ann wanted to ride along some more remote roads well away from main highways. The next day Ann rode her bicycle about 66 miles over nearly five hours. That night she asked if she could put a hammock up in our yard and sleep out of doors. That's the first time I ever remember having company sleep in our back yard in a hammock

Though their trip was shortened by Covid 19, we were delighted that Joy and her family took time to visit us during their trip back to this area.

My father's brother-in-law, Uncle Paul Fossum, Ida's husband, was one of the strongest men I ever knew. He had a gentle, caring spirit and a dry sense of humor. He could pick me up with one hand and set me on the platform of my John Deere Model B tractor or carry me anywhere.

When I think of Uncle Paul, I think of the time a severe thunderstorm came through and the hail it brought took out Dad's oat crop. At the time, Uncle Paul had a big Minneapolis Moline tractor. He brought over his tractor and a four-bottom plow and helped us plow up the oats field so we could plant soybeans as quickly as possible.

Uncle Paul's tractor wasn't my favorite green color, but I recall being so impressed with that big tractor.

As he got older, it was so difficult to see Uncle Paul's health decline after he had a stroke. He couldn't talk after that happened, which caused him a great deal of frustration. He had been such a large, strapping man. But his health continually declined as he aged.

I'll never forget the story my family told about him. Apparently three of his nephews – who themselves were not small people – were helping Uncle Paul haul hay bales. Just for fun, these nephews decided to take Uncle Paul down to the ground out there in the hay field. The young men would have been in their teens at the time. It was all in fun, nothing close to a personal attack. However, the three young boys couldn't get Uncle Paul down. As those boys got older, they were the ones telling the humorous story.

My mother's brother George Schmidt farmed a quarter of land with Dad. In their younger years, Mom and Dad, George and his family, Aunt Laura and their daughters Cinda and Carolyn, spent a lot of time together working and socializing.

Uncle George did his best to always remember Mom's birthday, which was March 11. One year Uncle George came over in a snowstorm because he didn't want to miss her special day.

Often, when he came into our house, he opened our refrigerator door and tease Mom. "What do you have for me to eat?"

Our extended family - aunts, uncles and cousins – were always close. We did our best to gather to celebrate everyone's birthday. Oma Schmidt always brought homemade angel food cake. She never used a boxed cake mix. Her angel food was made from scratch. Mom followed in her steps for a while, but eventually used boxed mixes. I guess baking an angel food cake from scratch is somewhat of an art.

I always loved driving Uncle George's Model 60 John Deere tractor and cultivated with it once. Its power steering was a treat for me, making the tractor so much easier to drive.

I always wanted to drive a mounted corn picker, which made it more difficult for me to get on the tractor. I had the opportunity to drive Uncle George's mounted picker once. Opa Schmidt rode with me. It was a fun experience.

For a couple of years, Uncle George played Santa for us kids at Christmas time. Everyone said George had a gift for gab, and he did a great job in his Santa role.

"Have you been good?" he'd ask. "I heard maybe you haven't been so good." We could recognize his voice, but he never acknowledged who he was while in this role.

Uncle George was known for playing pranks. I've been told I probably inherited some of that mischievous character from him.

When I married Rita, Uncle George couldn't resist the opportunity to tease me.

"Will you need a chaperon on your honeymoon?" I still miss my Uncle George, Uncle Paul, and Uncle Myron.

It was a thrill to be asked to be godparents to Tom Wiebesiek. His parents, Darwin and Susan, were our neighbors. In our younger years, Darwin and I had spent time together. For two years, Darwin and I farmed together. Unfortunately, with my full-time day job, it didn't work for me to try and do all my farming at night. Darwin didn't work off the farm, so he had the option to sleep in the next morning. If we were in the field till 10:00 or 11:00 at night, I still had to get up by 7:00 or before and go to work.

After we were officially installed as Tom's godparents at his baptism, Darwin and Susan and their two youngest sons, Adam and Tomm came over sometimes for a visit. Tom loved to play farmer, just as I had. It was a joy to bring out some of my childhood toys so both of us could play at farming.

When the boys were both small, I could go over the top of them with my wheelchair, which they thought was great fun. They lay flat on the floor, and I carefully rolled over them. One time Tom ended up with some grease on his shirt.

"Where did that come from?" his mother asked.

"Butch ran over us with the wheelchair," he said. The boys loved it and we all got a chuckle out of it. Not long afterward, the boys were too big to do that again.

All the boys liked to go deer hunting and fish with us, too. Rita and I enjoyed taking them with us.

One year we sent Tom a birthday card and Rita signed it Harlan and Rita. When Tom read it, he was quite dismayed. He had never known me by any name except Butch. "What happened to Butch?"

he asked his mother. She cleared up the confusion.

As they grew, we didn't see Tom or his siblings as often. Today Tom is a full-time farmer who enjoys livestock. He and his brother Josh farm together. Josh also has a trucking business. We just live two-and-a-half miles from each other, but busy lives seem to keep us apart.

Pictured from left to right: Back row - Rita, Arleigh, Ervin.
Front row - Harlan, Sophie, Joanie, and Ardie.

Great uncle and aunt George and Lena Symens, Joy's parents.

Arleigh and Sophie, 2007

Gathering for Mother's 96th birthday.

Rita's family - pictured from left to right:
Back row - Joseph, Bernard, Paul, Gene, Elmer, Donald.
Front row - Loretta, Mary, Edward, Rita and Ruth.

"And over all these virtues put on love, which binds them all together in perfect unity."

COLOSSIANS 3:14

TEN

DOUBLE BLESSINGS

Blessings have certainly been abundant in every area of my life. However, number one on that long list is the wealth of blessings my wife Rita brings to my life. And what a gift her family, the Bangassers, have been to both of us!

In addition to her twin sister, Ruth, Rita has one other sister, Loretta, and six brothers: Joseph, Bernie, Donald, Eugene, Paul, and Elmer. Rita was the baby of all. The very youngest. Her family always joked about how her parents always took the twins with them when they went somewhere to visit because those girls were so spoiled the brothers might have killed them.

Rita has maintained a diary since she and I married. That was something my mother always did. Over the years, the Bangasser family faithfully gathered for a family reunion every five years. The last one was the biggest family reunion. However, the reunion we held on Friday, June 28, 2013, brought the five-year cycle to an end. We are all aging and can't travel as easily as we once did. Because we knew that 2013 reunion was likely to be the last one, we made it count.

Family from both coasts came to South Dakota for the event. Rita's siblings, in-laws, nieces and nephews came from Texas and

171

northern Minnesota, Arizona, Ohio, Virginia, California, Colorado, Connecticut, Wisconsin, Oklahoma, and states in between.

The family gathering took me back to a fond memory about Rita's dad, Edward, who came to our house once for Sunday dinner. At the time, he lived on his farm with Rita's brother Paul and family. We had just been married for a short while. It seemed natural to have her father over for a meal. What we didn't know was that some of Rita's siblings had been inviting Edward to dinner for some time, but he always turned them down. Why he accepted our invitation, we'll never know. It was probably because we could talk farming. I always had a great relationship with Edward. He was a talker and I had no trouble listening to him as we discussed farming and all its issues. More precious memories.

Whenever Rita's family gathers here, they love coming to the farm to see the cows and calves, tractors and farm equipment, and the wide-open spaces. Family members who arrived on Friday came to the farm and we took tractors out of the machine shed for those who wanted to look them over or take a ride. At the end of the day, that gang joined Rita and me at Lennox Pizza Ranch for supper where we ate and visited well into the evening.

Saturday, June 24, we had arranged a catered meal at Saint Magdalen Catholic Church in Lennox. All together 98 members of the Bangasser family gathered for that meal. Many of the family couldn't attend. The ones who were there enjoyed visiting, a lot of good food, and took many, many photos!

Of course, there was plenty of leftover food from Saturday, so we all got together again on Sunday at Saint Magdalen's. For that day, we invited both extended Bangasser family members and some of the folks from the neighborhood where Rita grew up. We enjoyed a third round of visiting during lunch, then began sharing our farewells with those who were returning home.

Rita's brother Bernie, who has since passed away, was in a motorized scooter at that time. He was battling chronic obstructive pulmonary disease and was on oxygen. Despite his many health challenges, Bernie had not lost his love or zest for life. That's typical of the Bangasser clan.

Among my many fond memories of that reunion is the wheelchair/scooter races Bernie and I couldn't resist holding that Sunday in the church parking lot. Bernie, who served as a California policeman for many years, had faced multiple health challenges after nearly losing his life in a traffic accident.

Bernie was on duty and riding a motorcycle. To avoid colliding with another vehicle, he sacrificed himself and slid under a bus. The bus ran over his legs. You can imagine what he endured for several months as he recovered in the hospital. He underwent skin grafting, rehabilitation, etc. But Bernie was never a quitter. He and his wife had 10 children at that time. The 11th child was born while Bernie was still in the hospital. He was determined to do whatever it took to care for his family.

Bernie voluntarily retired after the accident. He could have taken a desk job, but that was against his nature. He also had to constantly stay active enough to maintain adequate circulation in his legs. It was only in the last years of his work that Bernie used a scooter to get around because his legs were failing him.

By 2013, chronic obstructive pulmonary disease made it necessary for Bernie to get around with a scooter. Throughout all those challenges, Bernie, like the rest of the Bangasser family, never stopped living as fully as he possibly could. He was definitely an example of how to live above your circumstances.

I don't think I will ever forget Bernie's first visit to our home shortly after Rita and I were married. It was about 1979 when Bernie and his wife Pat pulled into our yard with two vehicles. I watched in amazement as 11 children and Bernie and Pat piled out of those cars. It seemed like the stream of kids might never end.

Of course, the kids loved the farm and explored every nook and cranny. After being cooped up in a vehicle for such a long trip (from California), they were full of energy. My heart was in my throat a little bit when they climbed up onto the balcony of the old house we hadn't yet demolished on our farm site. As they hung over the railing, I prayed it wouldn't come apart.

After finishing our big gathering at church (and a scooter/wheelchair race), about 25 family members came to our home for a hayride.

It was a tradition for us to use a car trailer set up with lawn chairs instead of hay bales for our ride. We used our John Deere 630 to pull the trailer. Our nephew Carl drove it. Growing up, Carl always enjoyed helping Dad bale and hauling hay. During one of Carl's stays, he and Dad took time to do some fishing. Carl's brother Terry and sister Jackie wanted to get in on the fun too. They also spent some time at our farm. Since Carl was accustomed to driving a tractor, we designated him as our pilot for the hayride.

Even though hay wasn't involved in any part of this modern-day hayride, our flatbed trailer was loaded down with people! We used lawn chairs instead of hay bales. There were so many of us on that ride that a few people had to sit on the floor, there weren't enough chairs to go around. That didn't seem to bother anyone as we took a leisurely drive through Davis and back. The entire day was enveloped in a fun, lighthearted aura.

On Monday, a few relatives were able to share one more day with us. Our nieces from Connecticut came in the forenoon and had brunch with us. That evening, Rita's brother Elmer and his wife Mary hosted us at their Sioux Falls home as we completed this precious time of reminiscing and sharing before saying more goodbyes to family.

By Tuesday, Rita and I crashed! We were so thankful that we, Elmer and Mary, and Rita's brother Paul and his wife Vonnie, had taken time to make calls and all the detailed plans that brought so many of us together. We treasure the many memories made during that reunion.

One of Rita's sisters, Loretta, had a special connection to Rita and me. Loretta, in her later years, found herself living in Deer River, Minnesota.

For most of her life, Loretta suffered with rheumatoid arthritis. Despite the battles that disease brought to her life, I'll always remember Loretta's strong faith in God and positive outlook on life.

Over the years, Loretta had spent some time with Rita and me, staying with us for a couple of weeks at a time. As Loretta's 70th birthday approached, her children Mark, Karla, and Mary planned a weekend party.

On a Saturday, Elmer and his wife Mary traveled with Rita and me to Grand Rapids, Minnesota, where we met Loretta's family at a large motel. The facility featured a banquet room and café. It was common for couples to hold wedding receptions there.

We also met Rita's brother Gene and his wife, Marilyn, who traveled from Minneapolis. We gathered for a large party that began Saturday evening with supper at the motel. Throughout the evening we all enjoyed visiting and reminiscing.

Sunday morning we gathered again to attend church. Of course, we planned on having Sunday dinner together after church. Although the café was usually closed on Sundays, the owner, who was friends with Loretta, made an exception and opened for her and our family gathering. Loretta was so honored. To say the least she was delighted and so thankful, a typical "Loretta" response to life.

Nieces and nephews attending the Bangasser reunion; nephew Carl is driving the tractor.

*"For by me
your days will
be multiplied."*

PROVERBS 9:11

ELEVEN

THE HUNT

I n 1993 I had the privilege of being among the first hunters to take part in the Corps of Engineers Oahe Hunt at Pierre's Oahe Downstream Recreation Area, a 273-acre park on the west side of the Missouri River right below Oahe Dam. This hunt is held each year just for hunters who have a disability.

Among other accommodations, deer blinds for this hunt are built specifically with wheelchairs in mind. I'm told the success rate of these hunters averages about 60% each year. I am forever grateful to be among those who have had this special experience because, as a result, I held the record for about 20 years for taking the biggest deer here.

That first two-day hunt was scheduled to begin Saturday, November 13. We needed to travel to Pierre November 12, the day before the hunt began. The morning of November 12 was cloudy and the air was heavy. Our forecast for the day predicted that rain would move in and gradually transition to freezing rain, then snow.

That morning Rita and I went to our Davis insurance office to take care of a few things. By the time we returned home it was 11:00 a.m. A light mist was falling. We had a decision to make. Were we going to make the 240-mile trip to Pierre for this hunt? If so, we needed to get on the road right away.

Despite the weather we decided to make the trip. We were on the road for nearly two hours before the mist turned to rain. Just a few miles west of Chamberlain the rain turned to sleet. Our road, Interstate 90, was becoming slippery.

After another 40 miles, snow was falling and I-90 was slushy. We started seeing vehicles in the ditch. That was concerning, but it was too late to turn back now. We had less than 50 miles before we reached our destination.

As we drove, the snow became more intense, visibility was decreasing, and road conditions continually became worse. Shortly after we turned off I-90 onto Highway 83, which would take us to Pierre, we came up behind a snowplow. What a blessing! We were able to follow the plow all the way to Pierre. We had made our six-hour trip and were still in one piece. As we reached our motel, we thanked God for the safe journey.

That evening heavy snow continued to fall. We were scheduled to be at a 7:00 p.m. orientation meeting at Pierre's Corps of Engineers Maintenance Building at the recreation area. Needless to say, we didn't make that meeting.

We called the hunt officials, who advised us to stay put for the night and come to hunt the next morning as soon as we were able.

The following morning brought bright sunshine that reflected off 14 inches of heavy, wet snow. We gathered ourselves together and made it to the Corps building about 9:45 a.m. Our good friend, Mick Shevlin, met us there.

Shortly after we arrived, the Corps crew attempted to get Mick and me out to one of the deer blinds. However, the deep snow pushed up over the feet pedals of my wheelchair. Undaunted, the men kept working to advance toward the blind, until the belts on my chair came off. We couldn't move any further, so they parked me and Mick on a trail.

From there we did spot one nice buck. But again, the snow held my wheelchair hostage, and we weren't able to get me turned around so I could even take a shot.

178

Mick and I scouted for deer for about 90 minutes. Then one of the Corps team members took us back to the building for some good hot food. Once we ate, Mick and I asked for assistance to get back out to hunt. This time we were able to reach one of the blinds.

Three tiers of square hay bales surrounded each blind and sturdy plywood provided a solid floor. The plywood made it easier to maneuver a wheelchair. Blinds were set up throughout the recreation area. Ours was just off one road near an old, large tree.

We weren't in the blind very long before deer started passing through. I had a couple of opportunities to shoot at two- or three-point bucks and flat missed them. There were plenty of deer around and at least I was getting a lot of shots.

It was about 3:30 in the afternoon, while Mick and I were softly visiting, when the sound of a loud snort made our hair stand on end. We were certain a huge buck must have been less than five feet away. He was so close that we actually felt one of his snorts.

After recovering from our shock, Mick struggled to get me positioned in time to take a shot. We were both still a bit dazed. We never got a count of this big guy's many points, but he looked like a Christmas tree as he disappeared over a nearby hill. Mick and I stared at each other in amazement.

As the sun began to set at the close of the day, I still hadn't filled my tag. But I appreciated that I had shared the experience with my good friend Mick and enjoyed the beauty of God's wonderful creation as well.

A number of the hunters filled their tags that first day. One of them, Dick Lasagraard, shot a very nice 4x5, the biggest by far that was taken that day. Since Dick had bagged the trophy deer, he bought us all a round of drinks which we enjoyed as we ate our evening meal at the marina.

Sunday morning brought new hopes and expectations, with beautiful sunshine. Temperatures weren't excessively cold. As Mick and I patiently waited in the blinds, we spotted some nice does. They were in range, and I should have been able to take one. But Mick and I couldn't get my height adjusted quickly enough, or maybe I just plain missed the mark. A couple of times that morning things just didn't seem to click for us. Among other things, the trigger on my 22-250 rifle locked up on me.

When we came in for lunch, I learned a couple Corps of Engineers guys had given me a new nickname: Many Shot Harlan. I had done a lot of shooting the last couple of days, but no deer.

After lunch, most of the hunters were getting ready to go back home. Everyone, except me, had filled their tag. I seriously considered following their lead. Despite not bagging a deer, I had a great time at this first-ever deer hunt. I met new friends, including the Corps of Engineer crew, and other volunteers who assisted with the hunt.

As I visited with a fellow hunter, Greg Brander, I mentioned my inclination to call it quits. I'll never forget what Greg said to me.

"Harlan, don't hang it up just because everyone else has their deer and they're ready to go home," he told me. "You don't need to feel guilty about keeping the Corps crew here just for yourself. This is a two-day hunt, and the season isn't over yet. Go for it!"

I'm so thankful I followed his advice! Since my 22-250 rifle had given me trouble the first day of the hunt, Mick offered to let me use his 243. Since he had mistakenly brought the wrong shells for his rifle, his wife Elly made a quick trip into Pierre to get the 100 gram 243 shells we needed.

Once we had the ammunition, Mick and I bundled up again and Joe Hall, whom we really had bonded with, took us to a blind. By then, the wind had come up out of the northwest and was blowing around 25 to 30 mph. Conditions were bone-chilling cold. The deer were even staying under cover.

Initially, I had a couple of long shots, 400-plus yards. Needless to say, no luck with that. After about two hours of enduring the biting cold, I couldn't handle it anymore. I was in danger of turning into a completely frozen hunter. I instructed Mick to call in on our portable radio and ask the Corps guys to come and pick us up.

Some 15 minutes later Joe Hall and Lowell Somson showed up with the big Chevy Suburban. They put Mick and me in the back

180

seat and told us we had just a little bit of hunting time left. They were willing to drive us through the park and search for deer. Despite chattering teeth and shivering cold, I managed to say that yes, it was okay with me if we took a drive through the park.

"But please turn the heater on high!"

Time quickly closed in on us. We were down to about 10 minutes of hunting time left when Joe spotted a group of four or five deer. One of them was a buck.

Excitement began mounting when one of the guys said, "Oh, my gosh! It's the big one!" Thankfully, at that moment I didn't know how big the big one actually was. The guys quickly worked to get me set up for a shot. I tried with all my might to stop shivering long enough to get off a shot.

The buck stood behind two does. His rack was hidden behind a tree trunk. Another doe stood in front of his hind quarters. All I could see was his main body. That was probably a blessing. I may well have frozen stiff if I had seen his actual size.

As my three friends waited patiently for me to put the cross hairs of Mick's 243 Remington bolt action rifle on that mammoth animal, I steadied myself. Clearly this was my last attempt to fill my tag for this hunt.

I took aim and just as I pulled the trigger, the big guy took a step forward. My bullet struck him in the gut. Our excitement was intensely magnified! They guys started yelling, "You got him! You got him!" The buck went down about 250 or 300 yards from where he was hit. My friends knew they had to quickly finish the kill.

Lowell jumped out of the truck and Mick nearly took my trigger finger with him as he grabbed for his rifle. Every time these guys shot the buck, he jumped to his feet and took off again.

"Don't let him get to the river!" Joe was yelling at the top of his lungs. "What the __ is wrong with your shooting? Do I have to show you how to shoot?"

Just as the buck reached the riverbank, Mick placed a bullet in his neck. The big boy made his final fall into the river at a beach area. Mick and Lowell had to pull him out of the Missouri River.

The Big Boy was finally down. Now it was time to get pictures of my 5x6 250-pound, water-soaked deer that just missed being a Boone and Crockett (an objective measuring system used to recognize exceptional North American big game animals) animal by 6.30 points. I kept shaking with excitement – and probably from the cold. But I had just bagged one of the biggest deer in the area! He was the biggest buck I have ever seen before or since then.

Once we had the deer in tow, it was time to get back to the Corps building to continue the celebration and take more photos. The buck was a magnificent animal. I was advised to have him mounted. It was something I hadn't even thought about yet.

"You will have it mounted," my friends at the Corps of Engineers told me. At the time, it seemed I had little choice but to follow their directive. Now I know that, if I hadn't had the deer mounted, I would have regretted it deeply.

Back at the Corps building I completed the Corps hunt's tradition of eating a LITTLE – EMPHASIS ON LITTLE - piece of the raw liver of the first deer I had taken. It was a pleasure then to call my uncle George, who was in Pierre at the time visiting his daughter Carolyn and son-in-law, Doug Hofer. Doug was employed with South Dakota's Game, Fish and Parks (GF&P). My Corps of Engineer friends invited Doug to stop over and see the "little" deer I bagged.

Uncle George and I had a longtime habit of joking with each other and he pretty much knew my deer was anything but "little." Uncle George, his daughter Carolyn and her husband Doug came over to check things out.

After seeing the animal was a trophy deer, Doug asked Rita and I if we would stay one more night and agree to an interview with the GF&P director, who wanted to acquire some photos for their magazine, "South Dakota Conservation." Of course, we were delighted to accommodate that request.

"South Dakota Outdoors," a North Dakota magazine, and several newspapers also conducted an interview and took photos.

I'm blessed to have gone on many hunts since this first one.

Each hunt has been uniquely different and I'm grateful for all of them. This hunt, though, will always stand out as a special blessing.

Of course, I have continued hunting deer. One year I filled my Corps of Engineers Oahe Hunt tag early in the day. It was quite a contrast to my trophy deer, very small. After taking the deer, Mick and I went to Oahe Dam to do some fishing. When we returned for lunch with the rest of the hunters, my deer was displayed on a rack. A couple hunting "friends" decided it would be funny to spray white dots on the deer to make it look like Bambi. They went so far as to make it look like the deer had milk in its mouth. We laughed about it, although Mick thought it was a bit of a mean trick.

The thrill of bagging this trophy deer will remain with me all my life. I've taken several more nice deer over the years, but none that were close to the size of this buck.

"From the fullness of his grace we have all received one blessing after another."

JOHN 1:16

TWELVE

Outdoor Life

J ust because someone doesn't have the same physical capabilities as others doesn't mean they don't desire to do similar things.

Take hunting, for instance. I couldn't and still can't stand without assistance and would never have been able to lift a gun and fire it unless I had a device designed to hold the gun up while I pulled the trigger. But for as long as I can remember, I dreamed of hunting – and fishing. What a blessing that God put people in my life who didn't focus on what I couldn't do. They evaluated what I was capable of and found a way to design what I needed to enjoy these simple, everyday pleasures.

Dad often took me fishing as a kid, and frequently Opa, an avid fisherman, came along. There were times we fished all night, using lanterns so we could see our fishing rods and the fish. I'll never forget Opa, who would drop a sandwich and grab his fishing rod quick as a wink if he got a bite while he was eating. Dad and I weren't quite that dedicated. Unless a fish was pulling our rod down into the water, we finished our lunch break before we started fishing again.

It was common for the three of us to take off in the afternoon and keep fishing all night. Dad and I generally napped in the car for an hour or two during the night. But not Opa. He was right there on the shore, sitting in his chair. He may sometimes have fallen asleep in his chair, but he was wide awake and after the fish, if his rod wiggled at all. By mid-afternoon the next day, we were back home. Those are precious memories.

In my teenage years, I did the best I could to aim and shoot a rifle. However, without the aid of a device to hold my gun straight and steady, my chances of bagging any game were slim and none. I needed a gun holder.

When I was in my early twenties, my close friend Greg Schiferl designed and made my first gun holder. Essentially, the holder is a yoke. I fasten it to my wheelchair to rest my gun barrel in it. The holder has been so effective that I've continually used it over the years. While the base of the holder remains the same, some years ago, I had it retooled to add more functions.

In the years following my first hunt at Pierre, my fall hunting activities expanded, leading to some unforgettable adventures I still enjoy recalling.

One ritual that came out of the Corps of Engineers Oahe Hunt was fishing with Mick Shevlin while I was in Pierre. Every chance we had Mick and I went fishing. If Rita and I came to Pierre early enough to fish before the Corps of Engineers Oahe Hunt orientation and drawing for blinds began, Mick and I did some fishing.

One year, even though the outdoor temperature was zero, Mick and I headed to Oahe Dam on a Saturday evening after the American Legion and VFW meal held for all the hunters each year. It was midnight by the time we headed out. Rita told us we were both crazy, but we already knew that.

Because of the cold, Mick and I expected that many people who usually fished there would "wimp out," and we'd find very few fishermen on the dock, which is right below Oahe Dam. To our surprise, the dock was loaded with fishermen.

"Looks like a lot of wimps," I said.

Cold or not, Mick and I wanted to fish. We set our lines. Believe it or not, within the first 15 minutes, I landed a walleye, reeled it in, and Mick grabbed the line. As he reached for the line, the fish happened to touch the railing. Honestly, that fish stuck right to the railing bar. That's how cold it was! The fish started to wiggle, and we thought we were going to lose it.

Mick grabbed the walleye, pulled it away from the railing, released it from the hook, put it in the bucket, then looked at me.

"What do you think?"

"I think I'm becoming a wuss! It's just not going to get any warmer out here."

Mick agreed with my assessment, and we packed up and called it quits for the night.

It was about this same time that Mick asked me to join him in a hunt at Opal, South Dakota. Mick had traveled to the remote western South Dakota area for a few years and immensely enjoyed what he called his "Wild West" hunts. He had become friends with local ranchers Walter and Diane Fees, who operated a bed-and-breakfast near Opal called Juliet #1. Mick had shared some of my hunting stories with the Fees, who Mick said were anxious to meet me.

It all sounded like fun, but I knew I had to discuss the opportunity with Rita.

"You can either go hunting at Pierre or hunting at Opal," Rita told me. "You cannot do both."

I knew Rita was right, so I decided to do something different the following year and experience my own Wild West hunt at Opal. It proved to be a wise decision.

Opal is a spot in the road about 25 miles southwest of Faith, South Dakota. The bed and breakfast was located at the site of a former Minute Man Missile command center known as Juliet #1.

The Fees family owned the seven-acre plot before the federal government established the missiles in the 1960s. In 1993, when the missile sites were shut down, the family bought back the land and opened the B&B in 2006. Walter's mother, Faye, helped make meals at the B&B. (She and I still write letters back and forth and communicate by phone.)

The B&B features a TV room and hot tub, six decorated bedrooms, a restaurant, and a lounge. Visitors can arrange for a guided hunt during their stay or hunt on their own.

After our trip to Opal, while Rita visited with her twin sister Ruth about our experience, we learned that Ruth's husband, Patrick Marks, had been stationed at nearby Ellsworth Air Force Base, near Box Elder, South Dakota, during his Air Force career. Ruth said Patrick had sometimes manned Juliet #1 during his stay at Ellsworth. It's always a small world.

Hunting at Opal was quite a trip for Rita and me. After driving 240 miles to Pierre and another 130 miles northwest of Pierre, we left the paved roads and drove 25 miles on gravel to reach Juliet #1. Rita was so impressed (not). She was beginning to wonder just where we would finally end up. We had definitely traveled to a remote area. Our trip put us in a completely different time zone and seemed a very different way of life. Everything about Juliet #1 was relaxed. I immediately felt at home.

For our first visit to Opal, we expected our hunt to begin early the following morning. Walter wasn't a paid hunting guide, but he was willing to accompany us because he knew the area so well. He also served as our chauffeur, driving my van as we hunted. Rita and I wanted to be certain I was ready to go when Mick And Walter were, so we got up early. Once we were prepared, we made our way to the dining area.

We were surprised to find that the entire building was still dark. There was a couch in the dining room, and we heard snoring. As our eyes adjusted to the dim light of the room, we spied Walter, my hunting guide, sprawled out on the couch, sound asleep. Mick was nowhere to be seen. Rita and I exchanged puzzled glances, then sat and relaxed as we watched a beautiful sunrise.

Finally, Walter wiggled a little bit and started waking up.

"You up already?" he asked.

"Oh, yes," I answered.

He sat up and reached for the blue jeans hanging over the side of the couch, slipping them up over his underwear.

"Well, it won't be too long, and my wife will be here to start breakfast," he told us as he meandered toward the kitchen. Apparently, Diane had gone home to the ranch for the night.

It was getting close to 10:00 a.m. when Walter said, "I'll bet you guys want to go hunting, don't you?"

"Yes, I was thinking about it." I wasn't sure what to say. Mick hadn't said a word about hunts starting at midmorning, which really didn't matter to me. I'm not a morning person.

I'm happy to say that, despite the somewhat slow start, that day's hunt proved to be everything that Mick had promised.

Walter, born and raised in that area, was acquainted with most of the landowners there. He knew where we could hunt and who to call to inquire about hunting in a specific area.

Walter drove my van each day. I'll never forget some of the terrains we crossed. At one point, we left one main gravel road and drove 12 miles through several different pastures to another main road. None of the roads we traveled that day were paved.

In one place that was open prairie, we spotted an antelope herd. They had made their way over a nearby hill.

"Will your wheelchair make it up that hill?" Walter asked.

"Oh, yes!"

Thankfully, the ground was solid. I would have given anything if someone had been there to film us as we crept up that hill. It was a scene you might have found in many different hunting videos. We inched our way up that hill, checking every few feet to see if we could catch a glimpse of the antelope yet. Finally, we crested the hill, and the antelope took off like a shot.

We didn't fire one bullet before they were gone. Later that same day, we came across the herd again. We were up on a hill, and they were down in a valley. The antelope were easily 300 yards away.

"Wanna take a shot?"

I raised my eyebrows. "I've never shot anything that far away."

Walter said, "Go for it. Try it."

I followed Walter's instructions. Aiming for one of the antelope,

I pulled the trigger. The sound of the gun set the herd off again. Except for one. I had bagged my first antelope. What an exciting experience!

That thrill stayed with me for a long time. I was so taken with my accomplishment that, on a different hunt, I think I injured my eardrum when I shot the gun from in the van. When I saw another antelope herd, I got so excited I quickly fired four or five times. It was as if my mind went sideways, and all I could think of was getting that antelope, even if it killed me!

On our second Opal hunting trip, Mick and I hunted antelope and deer for a couple of days. Then Walter took Mick and me out on an afternoon turkey hunt. As we drove down a gravel road, a turkey flew onto the road right ahead of us. It landed, then took off, running right ahead of the van.

Another scene from the movies! Mick was hanging out the van window, using his 12-gauge shotgun to shoot at the turkey. After several shots Mick bagged the turkey. It wasn't long before we came upon several turkeys in a tree. The poor turkeys didn't stand a chance. All three of us went home with a bird.

2017 turkey hunt - about 12 miles from our farm.

Mick and I had the pleasure of hunting together at Opal for two consecutive years. Sadly, the following year Mick was diagnosed with cancer. Because of his illness, Mick was too weak to make such a trip. I sorely missed having Mick around but was thankful that Woody wanted to go hunting with me for the third year at Opal.

The third year we traveled to Opal, Woody and I were having a lot of fun, but my hearing was once again in peril. After I pulled that rifle trigger in the van several times, both ears were ringing. I could see Woody and Walter's lips moving. I knew they were talking, but I couldn't hear what they were saying. I began to recognize I was at risk for significantly damaging my hearing in my right ear. I must admit that the prospect of going deaf because of a hunt was frightening. After returning home from that hunt, a physician examined my ear and confirmed that my right eardrum was undamaged. Still, I don't believe I ever recovered 100% of my hearing in that ear. I had a new hunting rule: WEAR HEARING PROTECTION.

On one of the hunts that year, Walter set Woody and I up in a wheat field about 25 miles from camp. We were together in my blind, watching for deer while Walter went back to the ranch to get some work done. Woody sat on a folding chair in the blind, glassing for deer.

While we waited, we were having a good time. Woody was laughing about something and got so carried away he tipped his chair backward. He went flying right out of the back of the blind.

"Woody! No deer are going to show up here if you keep making all that racket." I had to give Woody a hard time.

A couple of hours later, the sun was beginning to go down. We started seeing deer come into the field in front of us.

I had a doe tag, and we got pretty excited when we spotted a deer coming straight toward our blind.

"Is that a doe or a buck?" Woody squinted every bit as hard as I did as we peered into the blinding glow of the setting sun to decide if I could legally shoot that deer.

"It's a doe." With Woody's confirmation, I put the crosshairs on the animal and pulled the trigger. The deer dropped to the ground. Woody sped toward it to check it out.

"It's a buck."

Now what? There was no way to reach Walter to seek his counsel. It was a thrill to take down a deer, but even though I hadn't purposely done it, I couldn't feel good about getting a buck when I had a doe license. Of course, if I had waited another 15 minutes, a nice doe came along.

When Walter finally came out to get us, he advised me not to be concerned about taking the buck. It was a relief to hear his thoughts on what had happened. Still, I wasn't certain whether or not I should contact Game, Fish, and Parks (GF&P). Thankfully I had a friend there I could consult with for advice on how to proceed. He worked in the GF&P office just outside Pierre.

After explaining what happened, I asked, "Am I in trouble? If I have to, I'll just leave the deer here. I won't bring it home."

My friend questioned me about the size of the buck's horns. By law, if the antlers aren't taller than the animal's ears, I was probably okay. By my measurements, the antlers were shorter than the buck's ears. Still, I had to jump through some hoops to be in the clear.

"Wrap the head in a plastic bag and bring it back with you and stop in my office. I'll measure it to verify its size," he told me. Before we concluded our conversation, I jokingly offered to share some of my deer meat with him. He laughed. After his inspection, I learned that I had been close to illegally taking the deer, but I hadn't violated the law. My friend Shawn, who would never pass up an opportunity to give me a bad time, made the most of the incident.

When it was all said and done, my friend said he was required to issue an official warning, which he mailed out to me. When it arrived, it was framed, and a note came with it.

"Your official punishment: you must hang this notice in your office."

Not all my hunting experiences were wonderful, but I must

admit the majority were adventurous. On one hunt at Opal, there were at least 500 pounds of mud clinging to my van when we returned to the B&B. We had gotten on some muddy paths, almost getting stuck at one point. There was so much mud on the van, you couldn't tell what color it was.

"What have you guys been up to?" Rita couldn't believe her eyes when she came out to help me get out of the vehicle. "You'll never get this van clean again."

"Oh, yes we will," Walter assured her. I don't know how many times Walter had to power wash that van at his ranch before the mud was finally cleaned off.

While I was out hunting at Opal, Rita took daily walks. Her stroll took her past an area where prairie dogs had dug holes in a pasture. Once in a while, Rita went off the road and walked past the prairie dog holes. As she shared her walking experience with us at a meal, Walter warned her it would be wise to steer clear of the prairie dog holes.

"A lot of times rattlesnakes hide out in those holes," Walter said. That was all it took for Rita to change her walking route.

One day we came across a little rattlesnake on the B&B driveway, right next to the gate. Walter bravely grabbed the snake, stuck it into a little container, and tossed it into the freezer.

"I collect snakes when I see them and preserve them so I can show them to people," he told us. Amongst his collection was a very large rattlesnake he'd kept in the freezer for a long time. I guess it was the safest way to show people a rattlesnake.

We were genuinely experiencing all the "wild west" had to offer. Deer, turkey, antelope, rattlesnakes, and more.

My hunting adventures weren't limited to four-footed animals. I enjoyed hunting geese, too.

One of my friends, Jerry Nelson, had a slough on his farm ground that he had landscaped to form an ideal goose-hunting site. He set it up so it was reasonably close to the road and relatively easy to access. One late afternoon in September, he invited me to come and hunt there with him. Another hunting buddy, Roy

Peters, came along.

Jerry truly knew how to stay out of sight when it came to hunting geese. He and Roy were dressed in camouflage clothing and were lying on the ground. Of course, there was no way I could get out of my chair to be beside them. The solution was to wrap me and my chair in burlap. Jerry had me wrapped up so tight that only my gun barrel was outside the burlap, and I could barely see through the burlap that covered most of my face. I was entirely out in the open. It was hard to believe any geese would land close to me. I felt I must stick out like a sore thumb at the slough.

The truth was that a lone goose – known as a bleeding-heart goose because it loses its mate at some point – came swooping in. It wasn't flying very high off the ground. I had never experienced being that close to a wild goose as it soared overhead. To me, it seemed like a 747 gliding over the top of us.

Neither Jerry nor Roy aimed at this bird. They were waiting for me to shoot because it seemed like a perfect shot for me to bag a goose. Without being too loud or doing anything to startle the goose, Jerry was whispering, "Shoot, Butch! Shoot!"

I didn't even hear Jerry. I was in a trance brought on by incredible disbelief that this beautiful big bird was just a few feet away from me.

I was so enthralled with the closeness of this huge bird that I never did shoot at it. I had never shot a goose in my life. As it flew away, Jerry sat up and gave me a stern lecture.

"What the hell is the matter with you? Why didn't you shoot?"

"I'm sorry," I said. "I was so overwhelmed with seeing that bird so close up."

"The next time I take you goose hunting and tell you to shoot, you better shoot. If you don't, I'm going to take you out of that wheelchair and kick you right in the butt." Of course, he would never DO that!

About one year later, I called Jerry and asked if I could come over to hunt that afternoon.

"Yes, you're welcome to come," Jerry said. "But it's 92 degrees.

I don't think there will be anything moving, but let's give it a try. At the very least, you and I can swap stories."

Jerry was a great storyteller, and he had a seemingly endless list of stories to share. I was more than happy to meet him at the slough about 4:00 that afternoon.

After getting situated in MY blind, Jerry and I talked quietly as we waited for some geese to stop in. Suddenly, Jerry stopped talking. "Do you hear that?" As he called my attention to it, I also heard the unmistakable squawk of geese. Jerry peeked out One of the blind window.

"There's two of 'em flying in. Sit still!" Both of us held our breath as we waited for those geese to find a landing spot. They made a nice big swing in front of the blind before landing right down in front of us. Just as the geese were ready to take flight again, Jerry whispered, "Shoot, Butch!"

This time I heard Jerry loud and clear, and I was ready to pull the trigger on my 12-gauge automatic Remington shotgun. Not only did I get one goose, I also got both of them with that one shot. Yes, that's right. The first time I ever shot a goose, I got two with one shot. It was pretty thrilling!

As excited as I was about getting the geese, I think Jerry was even more thrilled about it. I thought he was going to jump right through the front of my blind. He was so keyed up. Jerry stared in disbelief through the opening in the blind, then turned to me and started shaking me. "You got 'em, Butch! You got both of 'em!"

You probably have to be a hunter to understand the rush of emotion you get with this kind of experience. When I posted a picture of me with the geese on my Facebook page, some of my friends kidded me about the "tame geese" floating on the pond and sitting on the ground near the blind. Jerry had lifelike goose decoys sitting around us. They looked so real some people who saw pictures from our hunt that day thought the geese just flew in and sat right beside us. That's how realistic those decoys were.

I've never gotten over that thrill, and I'll always be thankful that God allowed me to bag those geese.

The decoys behind me in this photo look so real some people thought I was hunting geese that were just sitting around me.

Jerry was at least as excited as I was when I bagged two geese in one shot.

Roy Peters and I go back a long way. Roy was probably 16 or 17 when I first met him through a friend of a friend. We met after a church event in Lennox in my smoke-filled car. We were both smoking. He always teased me about being a bad influence in his life. Neither of us smoke today and we don't recommend it.

After high school, Roy attended veterinarian school at Iowa State University in Ames, Iowa. Because of his perfectionist personality, the pressures of vet school produced great anxiety in him. He set his standards high, expecting to consistently achieve certain grades. He put a lot of pressure on himself. Sometimes Roy called me at 1:00 or 1:30 in the morning, needing to vent some of his anxiety. After a couple of rings, Rita would simply hand me the phone and tell me, "It's your friend, Roy." We still chuckle about that. If I happen to call him late at night now, I know I don't have to apologize. "I know I owe you," he tells me.

After graduating from vet school, Roy worked as a veterinarian in Canistota, South Dakota. In his job he maintained a high standard of care for both the animals and their owners

Roy is the type of friend I can pick up with right where we left off, even if we don't see each other for months. Our relationship is one in which we are free to share whatever struggles we might be experiencing.

In the early years, we once went swimming at a gravel pit near Hudson, South Dakota. Roy didn't know how to swim, and I was using an inner tube to enjoy the water. Looking back, that was a risky adventure. It didn't take long for me to float the inner tube further out into the water than Roy could reach.

"Harlan, get back here," he yelled. "I can't reach you and I can't swim." I kept telling Roy I was fine, not to worry about me. We did some crazy things in our younger years.

We developed an annual tradition of fishing together. We fished many locations in southeast South Dakota. Generally, we caught fish, and we always enjoyed time together sharing our life joys, concerns, and faith in God. And I don't think there was ever a trip with Roy that didn't include some kind of crazy episode.

One time we decided to hunt ducks and located a slough we wanted to hunt. Roy wanted to get us as close to the water as possible because he knew he would have to use a ramp to bring me out of the van and over to the water. Turned out he backed up too close to the water and got stuck. We turned to each other and discussed how we were going to resolve our dilemma.

One of my cousin-in-laws, Dean, lived nearby. He rented the land where we were hunting. Maybe we could contact him for assistance.

"Let's hunt first and then we'll worry about how to get the van out," I said. We hoped to bag a couple of mallards but ended up with a mud duck, then called Dean who came with his tractor to pull us out.

This was just one example of Roy's determination to make things work for me and ensure that I had an enjoyable hunting or fishing experience when I was with him. It was a lot of work to use ramps to set me up to hunt ducks.

I have a friend, Rick Hurd, who lives west of Springfield, South Dakota. This man, who is also confined to a wheelchair, had built a handicapped accessible dock on the Missouri River. It was a great design and Rick quickly became one of my heroes.

One day, fishing on that dock, Roy and I were sitting and visiting, eating a sandwich. Roy had a little cheap fishing rod, nothing expensive by any means. He was always on the frugal side. It may have been something he picked up while he attended college and funds were scarce.

In the middle of our sandwiches, it looked like Roy might have a bite on his rod. It was wiggling. Roy grabbed the rod just as the string took off. He reeled and reeled.

"I think you've snagged a dead log," I said.

"No, I think I've got something," he answered. "Whatever it is, it came up out of the water just a smidge and I caught a glimpse of something pretty big."

The van was parked fairly close to the dock, so I told Roy he might want to get the net. He handed me the rod and ran over to grab a net, saying, "We have never caught anything big enough that needed a net!" While he was retrieving the net, I could feel that I was bringing the fish closer to shore. I reeled like crazy to keep it from racing away. More than once the strength of the fish nearly pulled the rod out of my hands. As soon as Roy returned, I handed him the rod.

"Here, you can break your own rod," I said.

For at least 20 minutes Roy wrestled with that fish. Finally, he brought it close to the dock, but it was definitely too large for the net. It was a paddle-fish.

"What have we caught?" Roy said. He had never seen a paddle-fish before. "I was almost ready to cut my line and let it go."

By grabbing the paddle, Roy got the fish up out of the water and onto the dock. Eyeballing it, we estimated that the fish was close to six feet long and weighed 65 pounds.

"If we don't take some pictures of this, no one will ever believe this fish story," I said.

We took many pictures, then put it back into the water. It was an exciting fishing trip!

Roy had never seen a paddle-fish before he caught this one.

Roy and I knew we needed plenty of photos of the paddle-fish or no one would believe our fishing story!

Not too many years ago, Roy and I went to fish at Lake Marindahl near Yankton, South Dakota. Shortly after we got set up, three young girls with kayaks came along and quickly went floating across the water in their kayaks. Pretty soon, a game warden showed up.

When he asked if we had seen the girls, we told him what we knew. He explained that the girls were under surveillance for drug possession and drug use. After he left, we wondered how long the authorities had been monitoring the girls. We didn't see the girls or the game warden for several hours, but as the girls returned to shore, the warden suddenly returned and arrested them after finding drugs in their kayak.

On the same fishing trip we met some neat people from Canada, a kayaking husband and wife, who were touring the

Missouri River and kayaking on nearby lakes. I became Facebook friends with them that same day. It was also that same day, on our way home from fishing, Roy and I nearly got caught in a tornado.

Roy and I still try to go on a fishing trip at least once a year. Every year we do something different. One time we had fish dinner before we ever threw out a line. Roy brought fish he'd caught before and cooked them on his camp stove. He really knows how to cook fish.

Roy and I have made many great memories and we're still fishing and building even more memorable experiences.

When he was first out of vet school, Roy came to visit us sometimes. One evening he helped Rita fry fish for supper. In his job at Canistota he was often on call, which meant there were times when he didn't get a lot of sleep. One evening while visiting us, he was so tired he laid down on the dining room floor and fell asleep. We couldn't wake him up for anything. Rita threw a blanket on him and we went to bed ourselves.

The next morning, we didn't even hear him leave. He was up

at 5:00 to head for Canistota so he could be there in time to go to work.

Roy and I share many memories. And we're still making memories. Close friends are one of life's best gifts.

Years ago I did a lot of shore ice fishing with Larry Flannery. His son Matt and daughter Melissa were always eager to go with us. She was a big help in making our lunches and getting night-crawlers for us. On one outing, the fish weren't biting. To stir up some excitement I pulled Matt and Melissa behind my wheelchair across the ice.

One of my "bucket list" items was an ice fishing trip. I ice fished several times in my younger years, right out in the open on a frozen lake. I was hardier then and could deal better with the cold weather.

Even though I wanted to ice fish just one more time, I knew it was unlikely that I would find an ice fishing shack that had a door wide enough to accommodate my wheelchair. Even if I did find someone with such a shack, if there was a lot of snow to get through, I wouldn't make it with the wheelchair.

If I were to go ice fishing, it would have to be done in a comfortable environment. I had seen a vehicle called a SnoBear on some hunting shows. I imagined how neat it would be to fish in a vehicle like that. But what are the chances that such a thing could happen?

The chances may have been slim, but God had it all worked out.

At the time, I was frequently receiving therapy at a medical clinic. Occasionally my therapist, Brian Iverson, had a physical therapy student assist with my treatment. I quickly learned that this young woman, Haley Lick, was from Rosholt, way up in the northeast corner of South Dakota.

"I was really young when my mother passed away," she told us. "Because of that, I've always been especially close to my dad. We've fished together a lot."

She described the SnoBear ice fishing vehicle her father owned, noting it was designed to give ice fishermen "all the comforts of home" while they were out on the ice. I literally could not believe my ears!

"I might have to get in contact with your dad," I told her. "Maybe I can hire him to take me ice fishing."

"I think that could be arranged," Haley said. That young lady was so gracious. She gave my phone number to her father, Donnie Lick, and sure enough, he called me.

After several phone calls, Donnie contacted me to obtain the measurements of my wheelchair. He had to make sure I could get into the SnoBear. Once we found that the wheelchair would fit, we set a final date to go ice fishing.

"Say, it's a long drive to Lake Travis," Donnie said. "Would you like to meet at a lake closer to where you live? I haven't fished that area much, but we could give it a try."

I wasn't concerned about driving to Lake Travis. If Donnie was gracious enough to host me on a fishing expedition, I was happy to drive the extra miles to meet him.

I needed someone to accompany me on this trip, and my neighbor Wayne Kuper was more than willing to drive me. Wayne and I left home about 7:30 in the morning to make the three-hour drive to Lake Travis. We met Donnie in a parking lot where he drove the SnoBear off his trailer. I used my ramps to navigate the six or eight inch height that took me right up into his vehicle. We left the parking lot and drove right onto the lake.

Donnie told us he had fished that lake nearly every day for years. He said he often finished morning chores at the farm and then went fishing.

"I don't even care if I don't catch a fish," I told him. "I'm just excited to have the opportunity to get out on the ice and be in comfort."

"Oh, we'll catch fish here," Donnie said. "No doubt about it."

Donnie wanted me to ride up front so he could give me any help I might need while I fished. To say the least, I was in seventh heaven. This trip was so far beyond anything I could ever have imagined. I was spending a day ice fishing! In complete comfort!

The SnoBear, which runs on tracks, had four holes we could use, and Donnie's electric drills zipped through some 20 to 21 inches of ice. Wayne sat at a hole behind me. As we settled into fishing, I noticed the SnoBear also featured two televisions and all the amenities anyone could want on a fishing trip. I don't think I could emphasize enough how comfortable we were while we fished.

I caught the first walleye, but it was too small to keep. It took about 10 minutes before we had another bite. Donnie used an underwater camera and other technology to see where the fish were. If we sat in a location for 20 minutes or more without a bite, Donnie moved the SnoBear to another location. We reeled in one fish after another. For the three of us, our walleye limit was 12. With Donnie's expertise and technology, we caught our limit.

"Now we'll go after some perch," Donnie said. By that time it was already 6:30 in the evening and the sun was going down. Wayne and I were still three hours from home.

"I love fishing, and I don't want to put a damper on this, but I think Wayne and I better call it a day," I told Donnie. I would have loved to keep fishing that day. I expected Donnie to be ready to go home by 6:30. But I think he would have fished half the night.

Again, the gracious host, Donnie was quick to respond to me.

"I certainly understand," he said. "If you guys want to take your fish and clean them at home, that's fine. Or follow me to my shop in Rosholt, about 12 miles north, I'll clean the fish for you."

Despite the late hour and the long drive ahead of us, Wayne and I quickly decided to take Donnie up on his offer. That was a smart move.

Donnie was an expert at cleaning fish. He had our catch cleaned, filleted, de-boned, and packaged in about 20 minutes.

It was 11:00 p.m. before Wayne and I got back home. We reflected on our day and thanked God for Donnie and such a perfect day of fishing. I was able to check off one more dream on my bucket list.

It's always so rewarding to see how God works things out in our lives, and sometimes in a big way. If I hadn't met Haley, it's likely, the trip would never have happened.

Since I was old enough to use a gun, I have always enjoyed hunting, including hunting pheasants. As I was growing up, I don't believe Dad and I ever missed the opening day of South Dakota's pheasant season.

The few times I've been able to bag a pheasant have been like winning the lottery for me. Since I'm not able to swing a gun, the odds of me hitting a moving target are not great. The most challenging hunting experiences I've had involve hunting pheasants.

In years past, I've attended an annual pheasant hunt held for veterans and guests by Birds, Bucks, and Berries at Parker, South Dakota. They start the day out by shooting clay pigeons, so everyone has a chance to polish their shooting skills. After that, we are treated to a lunch at their lodge.

When we're ready to hunt, they provide walkers and dogs and the rest of us act as blockers. I've always been intrigued by watching those hunting dogs work. My helper, Bart, from Parkston, used my "lazy susan" platform to help me turn and shoot at birds. I kept him pretty busy all afternoon, helping me turn and reload my semi-automatic shotgun.

Bart turning me on the "lazy susan."

205

The pheasant I bagged while hunting at Birds, Bucks, and Berries on a very windy day.

Me and Dad after a pheasant hunt in 1992.

After an afternoon hunt at our farm!
(L to R) Terry, Elmer, and Mary Bangasser.

Despite all my limitations, I've been blessed with an active hunting life, even bagging a turkey with a crossbow.

I'll always remember the day I went bow hunting during the Sioux Falls municipal archery deer hunt. This annual hunt, which also takes place in other large cities, helps manage the number of deer found in the city limits.

I'm certainly challenged to hunt with a bow. But I have always loved a challenge. As I waited patiently in the blind provided by the city, I was delighted to see a beautiful doe come into sight. Quietly I took aim and made my best effort to release the arrow. For a second, I thought I had hit the target. It looked like the arrow skimmed the doe's back. But my aim was off slightly. The doe bounded off, and I went home empty handed.

I couldn't resist sharing my story with another bow hunting friend who would take his own turn pursuing a deer in the municipal hunt. And I'm so glad I did!

He was fortunate enough to land a doe, and shocked to see that she had a scar on her back that looked like it could have been caused by the graze of an arrow.

"I'm sure it's the same doe," he told me. "You did graze that deer."

Just one or two inches lower and I would have had her!

One year John Weaver and I took these turkeys within three seconds of each other during a spring turkey hunt.

My dear friend Mick Shevlin and I with one
of the deer I took at a Corps of Engineers hunt.

"Every good and perfect gift is from above, coming down from the Father of the heavenly lights, who does not change like shifting shadows."

JAMES 1:17

THIRTEEN

God Connections

I f you share an extraordinary connection to some people in your life, you'll easily understand how devastated I was when my "adopted sister" Linda Flannery unexpectedly passed away in 2013.

Linda grew up on a farm outside Humboldt, South Dakota. She and her husband, Larry, and their children, Matt and Melissa, lived on an acreage outside Chancellor, 13 miles from our farm.

In her obituary, it was noted that "Linda loved to send cards that included her words of wisdom, advice, or a simple 'thinking of you.' She loved the color purple, butterflies, and angels – all symbols of the beautiful, strong woman that she was inside and out. She deeply cared for her family and friends – always having a smile and a hug for everyone."

That was certainly the Linda that Rita and I came to know. Perhaps her sensitivity to the needs of others stemmed from the loss of their son, Jeremy, when he was an infant.

Linda shared my love for viewing a stunning sunrise or sunset and gazing in awe at a marvelous moon as it slipped across a blue-black night. We called each other nearly every night to share our thoughts on the beauty of nature we were observing.

Linda's death was a shock to her family and everyone who knew her. It was the first day of September 2013. Early that evening, Linda gave us a call inviting us to share in a watermelon that needed to be used. Her thought was that it would be easier for her and Larry to bring the watermelon to our house than for Rita and I to get out. Rita was taking a walk when Linda called, but I knew she wouldn't mind having company.

We expected to see them drive into our yard before too long, but we waited for quite some time with no sign of them. Finally, Larry called and said while Linda was standing at the kitchen counter getting things ready to come over, she had collapsed onto the floor. She was out of his sight, and he was about eight feet away from her when he heard a loud thud. When he called her name, she didn't answer. He ran into the kitchen and found her lying on the floor. She didn't respond to his attempts to help her get up.

Larry called their daughter Melissa, a nurse, and told her he had summoned an ambulance and expected to bring Linda to the emergency room. When they didn't show up at ER, Melissa called us and asked what was happening. We had no idea. Melissa asked us to go over and find out, which we agreed to do.

When we pulled into Linda and Larry's yard, we saw an ambulance sitting next to their barn. No lights were flashing, and it didn't appear to be running. Our hearts sank as we began to realize something was very wrong. Both Rita and I were stunned.

Larry would tell us later that he believed Linda was gone before she reached the floor.

At the age of 59, it seemed a cruel twist that the life of such a loving, vibrant woman would end so abruptly. She was definitely as close as a sister to me. She gave the best, warmest hugs and had so many friends.

Linda, Larry, and the kids had become like family to us. She always helped me with my Christmas shopping for Rita. If either one of us had a bad day, we could talk it over and find support in one another. Linda and Rita worked together in church with the Catholic Daughters program. Linda was always such a hard worker.

212

If anyone needed help she was willing to step up and lend a hand.

She was also quick to share her faith in God. Outside of her husband, I was the last person to talk to Linda before she left this earth. It was a great honor to be one of her pallbearers. I'm not asked to do that very often. We still miss her today.

Larry and I still call each other several times a week and Melissa, who is very much like a niece to us, calls periodically. We have remained close, but we all have continued to experience an intense sense of loss.

One way I dealt with Linda's sudden death was to pour out the anguish in my heart in this letter.

To my dear sister Linda,

Oh, precious Linda. You left us far too soon. This just doesn't seem real. You had so many things to live for and so many people who still needed you. If only I could have taken your place, I would have done so in a heartbeat. But life doesn't work that way. Oh, to get one more, big hug from you, or hear your voice one more time.

Yes, I know when God calls me home, I will get that big hug and hear your sweet voice once again. I must be honest and say that I'm a bit jealous that you reached Heaven before me.

I told Rita this morning it would have made so much more sense if God had taken me instead of my sister. But God's ways and plans are obviously not ours. Deep down I know His ways are always right and perfect. I still told Him I thought he really messed up on this plan. It just isn't fair, it really sucks.

How I'm going to miss those phone calls we so often made between 10:30 and 11:00 at night. Calling each other to look out at the beautiful moon, especially the full moons. Or in winter when you were driving to work and called to share your appreciation for a gorgeous sunrise. Oh, how you loved the beauty of God's nature, and you were always eager to share that passion.

I will always cherish those shopping excursions when you helped me select gifts for birthdays, Christmas, and anniversary gifts for Rita. Your husband Larry had to run scrimmage so Rita wouldn't see what we were buying. Sometimes, you picked up a gift for Rita, taking a picture of it so you could ask for my input.

We had fun times in Bath & Body Works, inhaling different fragrances, going out to eat, or sharing day trips. With your big smile, caring spirit, and positive attitude, it was always a joy to share a day with you. It was clear that you loved life, your family and friends, and you were always ready to help someone.

It was also fun to tease you, Linda, as you took it so well. As a brother I felt that was one of my duties.

Do you remember, when you were home alone, and I'd tell you, "Good night. Don't the boogie man get you." You always scolded me. "Harlan, don't say that. It's not nice." That was rather mean on my part, but that's how brothers can be.

You always gave me heck if I'd be at the office and didn't tell you, cuz we might have been able to have lunch together, which as you know, we sometimes did. Then the times I wouldn't get my phone answered, you'd say, "Harlan. This is your sister, Linda. Are you screening my calls, or are you mad at me?" And I would do the same to you.

Then there's picture taking at different events. We both believed you couldn't take just one picture of a subject. You had to take at least three or four. By the way, who's going to help me take pictures now?

Oh, I almost forgot to tell you. Rita came across that little memo pad with the butterfly on it that you gave her. When she read your note saying, "Rita, thank you for being such a good friend," she cried, knowing it came from your heart. You were always thinking of others.

I want you to know I really did appreciate all those little things you did for me. I will also cherish forever those phone calls we had, being able to share the day's events or frustration and not having to worry about how it sounded nor to be judged.

Sister Linda, I'm going to miss you so very much, and so will many, many others. I think of how torn I am, and think of how much more torn your dear husband, son, daughter, son-in-law, and granddaughters are. But even though we grieve, we need to make your passing a celebration of your life. We know you are in the presence of Jesus, enjoying all the wonderful and beautiful joys of Heaven. You're with Jeremy and other family members. I'm sure by this time you've received lots of hugs from my sister, Joanie.

We know God will give us the help and strength to get through this dark time. He gives us the promise that, if we have Him in our hearts, we will be gathered up to Him and be reunited. The best is yet to come. What a glorious day that will be!

I love you, sister Linda.

Your brother,
Harlan
P.S. I will always look at the moon in yet a more special way knowing you are on the other side, viewing it from Heaven. And watermelon will taste just a bit sweeter.

Some of my closest friends (left to right): Melissa Flannery Plucker, Linda Flannery, Melissa Skaff.

Rita and I shared the joy of Melissa Flannery Plucker's wedding.

One of the birthday celebrations we shared with Melissa and her family.

Rita and I have made many great memories with the Flannery family. Pictured here with us, Linda Flannery and Melissa Flannery Plucker.

"A friend loveth at all times, and a brother is born for adversity."

PROVERBS 17:17

FOURTEEN

I REMEMBER WHEN

Thank you to all who shared a special memory that I can include in my memoirs.

SHELLEY YOUNG

I believe that, from the day I was born and the first time I met my uncle Harlan, we were special to one another. It didn't hurt that I was born two days after his birthday!

"Unk" has continued to be special to me throughout my life. I have so many memories of visits to the farm as I grew up. Unk always had fun activities planned for us. Our favorite thing to do was bring the antique John Deere tractors out. Both Unk and I loved the sound the tractors made as we ambled down the road.

My dear Unk talked Rita and I into securing him to the tractor with a bungee cord. Once he was secure, standing on the tractor's toolbox, away we went. The good Lord was certainly watching over us that day and many other times over the years.

When Unk got his new motorized wheelchair, things changed. He had so much more freedom to stretch out, move his feet and legs, and elevate to get closer to any type of table. The chair could travel up to 8 miles per hour! Unk had to try out his new chair, which was equipped with wheelie bars on the back. He wanted to see if the bars would actually keep him from tipping over. To test out the chair, he went ditching. I followed behind him just in case. The bars successfully kept him upright.

We experienced another change when I got my driver's license. Over the years we've had many road adventures. I remember visiting one of his friends, who wasn't home when we stopped in. So we (I) moved one of the guy's grain trucks and made a big heart on his front step with a piece of coal so he would know we had visited.

Unk and I also made a couple of trips to the University of South Dakota Gross Anatomy department. Very educational!

On one adventure we visited Yankton's old bridge, placing "Love Locks" (padlocks) on the bridge in memory of our loved ones who have passed away.

Our favorite place to visit is Falls Park in Sioux Falls. Over the years we have watched the park transform. It's now much more handicap friendly and so relaxing as we sit and listen to the water rush over the rocks.

Once my dear Unk crosses the rainbow bridge, completing his earthly journey, I have a necklace to hold some of his ashes so I can take him on many wheelchair-free adventures!

Unk's special niece, Shelley Young

PASTOR HARLAN HAYUNGA

I am honored to be part of your journey. My reflections include driving your John Deere A on hayrides, managing to drive the tractor even though the hand clutch was on the "wrong" side for a left-handed person. I recall fishing trips with you and Marlin, and the fun and fellowship we enjoyed regardless of whether or not we caught any fish.

There were also the unscheduled times Verlaine and I met you and Rita on the Sioux Falls bike trail as we relaxed, visited, and watched the water go by. We jokingly said we were having a short vesper service.

You and I had many meaningful conversations in church, during Sunday School and over the phone. You were always eager to listen and learn. You were attentive to words such as predestination, election, and the sovereignty of God. You live a life of grace and bless others by your faithful witness.

REGINALD WOOD

I first met Harlan at his office in the winter of 1972. After introducing myself, he greeted me with a stern look. He tossed his driver's license across his desk, then informed me that he had requested financial assistance from the State Vocational Rehabilitation Agency, where I had recently been hired. My supervisor had responded to Harlan's request that, due to the severity of his disability, Harlan shouldn't/couldn't drive an automobile. Harlan asked and received a loan from a neighbor to purchase a used car. He tracked down a used, discarded hand control which his dad and another neighbor installed in his "new" car. He then passed his driver's exam and was issued his driver's license. I was very proud to be Harlan's best man at his wedding!

RHONDA RIEBELING

Harlan and I have a looong history. Our friendship began in the mid 1970s when a friend of mine, Donna, attended a singles retreat at Inspiration Hills. She met Harlan at the retreat. They became fast friends because they both had disabilities and both liked to smoke.

When another retreat was scheduled, Donna convinced me to attend. I don't recall being introduced to Harlan or the content of our first conversation. However, one distinct memory I have of that evening is how several men at the retreat brought Harlan to the lower level of the main building at Inspiration Hills. If you're familiar with that building, there are many steps to the lower level. Since there was no elevator in the building at that time, three or four guys helped pick up Harlan and his wheelchair and carried him to the lower level.

As I watched, I thought how trusting Harlan must have been. He looked so calm. Later I learned that he was actually quite nervous about being picked up and carried. But how else could he have gotten to where the action was? Thank goodness for the Disabilities Act that makes facilities like these so much more accessible now.

After that first and then a second retreat, Harlan, Donna, and I became friends. Eventually, Rita joined us, too. I called us Harlan's Harem. We still laugh about throwing grapes at Harlan to see if he could catch them in his mouth. He was successful in that once or twice.

Somewhere along the line, our core group began celebrating New Year's Eve together. In the early years, a few from the retreats joined us. For the most part, though, it was Harlan, Rita, Donna (until her passing) and I who gathered to celebrate many New Year's Eves. However, Harlan did threaten to throw me out of the group after I missed a couple of times.

My New Year's memories include: drinking amaretto and hot chocolate (Harlan's having a "little" more amaretto than mine) and then asking him to say grace before we ate; walking and rolling over bubble wrap to make popping sounds like firecrackers and shooting off fireworks New Year's Eve 1999 into 2000. We had many, many laughs while playing Taboo, Harlan's (not) favorite game.

In our single days, Harlan did his best to introduce me to single men. I recall a meal at Harlan's home with a truck driver (I think). Another guy brought Harlan to Sibley where the guy was struck by the sign posted above a local church: "Prepare to Meet Thy God." If I recall correctly, this gentleman wondered if there was something in the local water because we all got the giggles when we went to get something to eat.

Harlan's favorite memory is the evening we double-dated and Harlan drove. The date Harlan invited for me was rather timid. When he stepped away from the car for a few minutes I asked Harlan, "Does he thing I have the plague or something?" We don't recall how Harlan answered me, but as we were parting for the night, Harlan said something like, "Rhonda, come here and give me a kiss so you get a goodnight kiss!" Harlan thought that might give my date a hint, but it was to no avail.

Harlan is one whose attitude is to "live life." He maintains a bucket list. Once he discovered that my husband and I lived close to Iowa's former high point and current high point, it was his goal to visit both locations. One summer day we all set out to climb the former high point, a mound. The going was good at the outset, but about two-thirds to three-fourths of the way up, the incline became too steep for Harlan's chair. He was bummed. Even with Rita and my husband helping push, it just wasn't going to happen. We made our descent, but my husband and I were inspired by Harlan's effort. He tried. You may not succeed but try. Who knows what beautiful view you may see?

Harlan and I have shared many laughs, but what has touched me more are our conversations and the support we give one another during difficult times. When my brother passed at an early age, Harlan, Rita, and their friends Larry and Linda, traveled 60 miles to come to the visitation. Harlan was asked, "Do we know this guy?" His response was, "We know Rhonda."

What a heart of compassion, showing his support and how much he cared. When our mutual friend, Donna (who brought us together) passed, Harlan and Rita traveled those 60 miles again for visitation. Afterward, we shared memories and celebrated Donna's life with root beer floats.

The most difficult experience Harlan and I have shared was the passing of his best friend and my good friend, Linda. She died very unexpectedly. I remember kneeling by Harlan's wheelchair at the cemetery, both of us weeping and talking as our spouses stood at a distance. Once again, we had lost a very dear friend.

Perhaps it was these losses and our advancing age that initiated our deeper conversations. I remember one of our talks took place when we met Harlan and Rita at Grand Falls Casino. We dined together and dropped a few quarters in some machines. Then we all wandered out to the swimming pool. Harlan indicated that he wanted to talk to me, and we had a rewarding conversation about heaven. Who would have imagined that could happen at a casino?

Our conversations have turned into an hour long walk on a bike path and two-hour visits on the phone. The range of topics is immense, spanning health concerns, friends and family health concerns, recalling memories, laughing, topics I can't/won't mention here, and teasing each other, to serious talks about Jesus our Lord, dying and heaven.

The real thing that amazes me though is God's providence in our relationship. Never in my wildest dreams did I think when they carried Harlan down those steps that we would be friends nearly 50 years later. Nor did I think or even dream that I was going to meet my best male friend, my inspiration, the best listener and supporter, and my prayer warrior. And when I think that God, through Donna, and through Harlan, has led me to some amazing friends, I am awed at what a tapestry God has woven. I am very privileged and thankful for knowing and having such an awesome relationship with Harlan. I didn't deserve to be this blessed, but I am so, so thankful that I am.

LARRY RIEBELING

The first time I met Harlan was in 1992. At that time, he and my wife-to-be had been best friends for a long time. Once Harlan found out I had a farm background, a soft heart for John Deere tractors, and that I was an agronomist, he and I pretty much hit it off right from the start.

We quickly established an annual tradition of visiting Harlan and Rita on or around Labor Day. While we were there, Harlan appreciated having me take yield estimates of his crops.

Rita usually took a break while Harlan, Rhonda, and I headed out to the field on his John Deere ATV. In early September, a corn field isn't the most pleasant place to be. It's hot, tassels fall down your neck, and dry corn stalk leaves tend to cut into your arms and face.

While I made my assessment, I heard Harlan and Rhonda laughing and talking, having a really good time. Each time I finished one area, Harlan looked into his seed book and directed me to a different variety 24 rows away. After completing several yield checks, I was pretty hot, sweaty, and dirty. I kept thinking we must be finished and ready to head to the yard for a cold beer. That's when Harlan told me we had to head toward a second field. I'm starting to question whether or not I really like this guy. But the truth is, it's impossible not to like Harlan.

We traveled to the second field, where I completed the same yield check. Boy, am I looking forward to that beer! Not yet though. Harlan asks me to yield check the soybeans.

Anyone who's walked into a soybean field in September knows it's not a picnic. The soybeans grow into each other and just walking in the field is difficult. I'm from northwest Iowa and used to 30-inch rows, but Harlan planted his soybeans on 20-inch rows, making my job even more challenging.

All the while I'm working, I hear Harlan and Rhonda laughing and having a great time. I'm starting to wonder if they are already enjoying a beer without me. After several hours I finally finished the job. Truthfully, if anyone but Harlan had asked me to do this, I would have told them to go jump into a lake. But can you say no to a nice guy like Harlan? When we finally returned to the yard that beer tasted really good.

Harlan definitely hasn't had an easy life being confined to that wheelchair from a young age. On the other hand, Harlan has had the opportunity to do so many things that most people in wheelchairs cannot even dream about. This is due to a number of things. One of them is Harlan's personality. If Harlan says "Hello" to anyone it turns into a conversation, and then to friendship. Because of his outgoing personality he has so many friends, who are willing to do anything for him.

Above all, Harlan has a wife who is an angel on earth. Rita's love, devotion and hard work are beyond words. If anyone deserves a special place in heaven it has to be Rita. Harlan's life would be much different without this wonderful woman. Once you meet Harlan and Rita, you have to love this wonderful couple. What an outstanding example this couple is to all of us. I wish them the very best in the future.

SUSAN CARLSON

So many memories come to mind when I think of Harlan and Aunt Rita's life together. Since I didn't know Harlan before he and Aunt Rita started dating, my recollections only span the last 44 years.

One clear memory I have is the day Harlan and Rita came to visit us. We lived on the farm near Renner with Grandpa (Rita's dad) and Ed (her brother).

After we visited a while, I was sent to the garden to water the tomatoes. That job consisted of filling five-gallon buckets of water and hauling them in the back of the pickup out to the field where the garden was, in the midst of the corn and hay fields.

Harlan wanted to see our garden, so he and Rita drove Harlan's van out to the field as I bounced along in the pickup with my load of water.

Once we arrived, we visited while I started watering tomatoes. Very casually Harlan asked me what I thought Grandpa would think about he and Rita getting married. It didn't take me much time to respond.

"Do you love Rita?"

"With all my heart."

"Rita, do you love Harlan?"

"I do."

As worldly as a sixth-grader can answer, I told them, "If you love each other, then that's all that matters and Grandpa should be happy you have each other."

Harlan looked at Rita. "Well, okay then," he said.

That was it! We drove back to the farm. Dad was milking cows and we all had chores to do. Harlan and Rita went back into the house, then left a short while later. It wasn't until the next day that

Mom told us Harlan had asked Grandpa for his blessing to marry Rita. NOW it hit me about our conversation at the garden and how important it was for them. And I just thought we were watering tomatoes.

I also remember watching Harlan do cookies in the church parking lot, coming home from Pat and Tammy's wedding in your van during a rainstorm as I sat in a lawn chair in the back. I recall Harlan conversing with mannequins in a store at the mall and walking down the aisle with Joel for your wedding.

One of the years when I was in 4-H, Uncle Harlan called and told me he had a heifer that was pretty nice. Would I like to come and see it?

Me and my parents loaded up the trailer and headed to Harlan's farm. One look and I knew that this Simmental heifer, Harriet, was going to my farm. She had that "show heifer" look and she was going to be mine for the summer. I couldn't wait to love and care for her.

Harriet was so cool. She was gentle and fun to work with and to show. Harriet and I went to the county, state and open class shows throughout the summer. Now it was fair time at Rock Valley, Iowa. Uncle Harlan, Rita, and I loaded Harriet in the trailer, hitched the trailer to Harlan's van, and off to Rock Valley we went. I'm quite sure it was the first time anyone saw a conversion van hauling a cattle trailer to a show. That didn't stop us. No one was laughing at the end of the show when we drove away with our Reserve Champion Breeding Heifer!

Next stop was the Sioux Empire Fair (in my county). On the day of the show, Harlan wanted to get closer to the show ring to take it all in, but the boards around the ring blocked his view. So, as I entered the ring with Harriet, Rita pulled Harlan up out of his wheelchair and propped him up along boards of the show ring. There he dangled, holding on as Rita held him up. We won our class. Now it was time to pick the Show Champion.

All the other heifers came into the ring, and we paraded around the ring. With each pass we made, Uncle Harlan slipped lower and lower on show ring board. Finally, the judge selected Harriet as Champion Breeding Heifer. Rita helped a very excited Uncle Harlan back into his chair! Harriet and I also competed in showmanship that day and won the Junior Division. We celebrated a the 4-H snack stand.

Harriet and my final show was at the South Dakota State Fair. Uncle Harlan and Aunt Rita were unable to attend. Harriet and I were at the show ring for what seemed a very long time. Classes came in and out, and we waited.

Finally, after my mom realized that the class I was to be in was already done, the ring check-in staff talked with the judge. I was allowed to enter the ring. I led Harriet around the ring once, set her up, and that was it. The judge took the microphone and explained to the audience that we were to be in the previous class and stated that we definitely deserved a purple ribbon. My first purple ribbon at the State Fair!

We were also chosen to be in Showmanship where we placed in the top 5. After the show, once Harriet was safely in the barns, I ran to the fairgrounds pay phone and called Uncle Harlan and Rita to tell them the good news. It was a bittersweet end to a great summer with Harriet. My time with her was done. Shortly after we came home, Harriet went back to Harlan's farm to be a momma cow. I will always be grateful for the opportunity to share these experiences with Harlan and Rita.

But most of all, I remember the unconditional love that you had with your parents and Joanie. And that love extended to all of us. So many conversations . . . and I cherish each one!

PATTY SINNING

My cousin Harlan, or as we always called him, Butch, has always been an inspiration to me. Always up for an adventure, and eager to try anything. We shared those family Thanksgivings and spur of the moment hay rides with his B John Deere humming down the road. Later it was road trips to weddings, where we enjoyed a dance! Locomotion is his favorite dance tune. He was always in the lead in the "family conga line." He never gets tired.

Butch loves to capture moments with his camera – or your camera. Which I can really appreciate. I think he invented the selfie. I wonder how many pictures he actually has.

He is probably one of the best conversationalists I know. He is quick to engage an unsuspecting victim to find out all about them. All kidding aside, Harlan loves to meet people. He cares about people. His interested in you. Like writing a letter or thank you note, the art of conversation is truly a gift. Which means Butch is also a good listener. He seems to know everyone.

After I was married, I joined the church where Butch grew up. I knew his faith was important to him, but I saw it firsthand as he interacted with others, especially visitors. I think he inherited that "welcoming" gift from his mother, Sophie. She in my eyes, was the unofficial greeter for the church.

We both watched our parents age and require different levels of care and attention. Butch was a great son, always working hand in hand with Rita to be good advocates for their parents' needs, and for Joanie's needs. A good Christian upbringing was certainly the foundation.

KATIE SCHRAMM
Sometimes people come into our lives under ordinary circumstances but have an extraordinary impact. Harlan is one of those people. I met Harlan when I was a senior in college. I had planned to become an Occupational Therapist (OT), and was in the University of South Dakota's OT program. One of my professors thought an opportunity to meet Harlan and his wife, Rita, and learn more about Harlan's daily routine and how he and Rita accomplished daily activities would be a good experience for me. My professor introduced us via email, and the rest, as they say, is history.

Recently, Harlan reminded me of the first time I came to their home. I had forgotten the exact details, but recalled all the feelings that surrounded our relationship from the beginning. I remembered instantly caring about Harlan and loving him, just from emails and phone conversations. He has that kind of energy. Remembering those feelings, his description of the first time I walked in the house makes total sense.

I walked in, introduced myself, and gave him and Rita a hug. During that first visit, I also apparently shared with both of them that they were now considered part of my family forever, whether they liked it or not. Now, there are people who are prone to hugging and extremely loving. I am not generally one of those people, unless I'm sure that the person on the receiving end reciprocates the feelings. I must have sensed that we were all instantly bonded and connected enough that Harlan and Rita would indeed be part of my family forever.

One of my favorite experiences with Harlan was a visit to Falls Park in Sioux Falls, South Dakota. My fiancé, Mason, and I met Harlan and Rita there. We wandered, talked and took pictures of course! If you know Harlan, you know that he loves pictures. It was such a simple experience, but it was also memorable in many ways.

The Falls were beautiful, as always. The weather could not have been nicer. The conversation flowed so easily that we didn't even notice the passing of time. It was the first time Harlan met Mason, despite each of them hearing many stories about the other. Truthfully, I couldn't have scripted a better evening. What's remarkable about the whole encounter is that I had only known Harlan for a couple of months at this point, yet it played out as if we truly were a family.

The time we spent together in a "formal" sense was short, just a couple of months. But we are still closely connected 10 years later. Harlan and Rita came to my wedding, and Harlan and I shared a couple of the best dances of the entire night. We kept in touch even when my husband and I moved to West Virginia. We reconnected when Mason and I moved back, and now we are blessed to be able to share our special friendship with our two-and-a-half-year-old son, who said it well: "Harlan is fun. Can he come play with me again? And Rita can give me a hug!" If that doesn't say it all!

DONETTE WHEELOCK

As Harlan, Rita, our employee Jared, Greg and I approached a Lake Okoboji dock on a cool, overcast morning, our anticipation ran high. As owners of Crop Insurance Services, Greg and I had worked with Harlan and Rita through their temple Insurance Agency for several years. As is typical with Harlan and Rita, the business relationship morphed into a friendship. As Harlan shared stories about his hunting and fishing adventures, we decided to treat him and Rita to a weekend stay at an Okoboji resort for a new fishing experience.

Our plan to fish the first night we were there was thwarted by a thunderstorm that brought heavy rain. So, we all settled for a pleasant meal at the resort, card games, and conversation. The next morning, our guide and captain were just pulling up to the dock to take us fishing for the day. There was a bit of maneuvering to get Harlan in his motorized wheelchair safely on the pontoon. Then the rest of us piled on and headed out.

The plan for the day included dropping Rita and me off on shore at some point, however that didn't happen. Rita and I stuck with it and napped if we became bored.

Always available to his insurance clients, Harlan fielded a business call while we were on the lake. Now that's customer service!

Despite the rain, the weekend was a success. The guys did catch fish to bring home. Before we parted that memorable day, with a fish story or two and a stronger friendship, we presented Harlan with a t-shirt that read, "Even Jesus had a fish story."

We so admire Harlan and Rita with their loyalty to friends and family, their sense of fun, can-do attitudes, strong faith, work ethic, and integrity. Even though we're all retired now, we stay in touch, and we've enjoyed following Harlan and Rita's adventures on Facebook. Harlan and I have had many conversations about end of life, faith, and our shared experiences as hospice volunteers. We are grateful for their friendship and Harlan's mischievous smile is a constant reminder to seize each moment, find adventure, have fun, and live each day fully. Carpe diem!

"And God is able to bless you abundantly, so that in all things at all times, having all that you need, you will abound in every good work."

2 CORINTHIANS 9:8

FIFTEEN

ADVENTURES AND SMALL PLEASURES

When I was in my late teens, Pastor John DeYoung and his wife, Dorothy, served our church for three years. He grew up in Springfield, South Dakota, 75 miles from Davis. In addition to being a great Christian role model and a man of God, Pastor John had three attractive daughters and one son, all of which made it easy to often hang out with the family.

Pastor John was great for my self-esteem as he was always encouraging me to step out and try new experiences. He, his wife, another couple, and I took some road trips together, including a visit to the Shrine of the Grotto of Redemption in Iowa. During the time they were here, I felt like they were part of my family, and I was part of theirs.

I was probably 19 when Pastor John insisted that I attend church camp that summer along with the other youth at Lake Okoboji.

"You're going to camp, aren't you?" he asked.

"That's not possible."

"Why?"

"I need someone to help with my personal care."

"That's not a problem, you're going," he said. I'm forever grateful that I listened to Pastor John and attended camp. He was the one who was there for me every time I needed some help. And I had a riot. The camp events were very inspiring and all of it was just plain fun.

I also have to chuckle about Pastor John's advice to me about my smoking habit. He advised me that I would not be able to smoke while I was at camp. Most of the time I was there, I didn't smoke. But the day before camp ended, I ran into some other young people who'd been hiding over a big hill all week to enjoy their smoking habit.

I had to ask, "Where were you guys the last five days?" I did enjoy some smokes with them the last two days I was there.

One of my friends at camp that year was very popular in high school. He could easily get a date. Red-blooded American teens that we were, we teased each other and had some friendly competition, even about dating, and I did have a date.

On the way home from camp, we stopped at Arnold's Park. My friend dared me to ride the old wooden roller coaster there. I was hesitant. I wasn't sure that was a good idea.

However, my friend persisted, and I thought, "I don't want to be beaten by anyone." So, I agreed to the ride. I was really surprised when he got sick. I felt bad for him, but told him, "I'm going to ride it again."

I was heartbroken when Pastor John and his family moved back to California, where Dorothy grew up. I was losing one of my best friends.

When Pastor John and Dorothy returned to the area for a visit, they loved to surprise me. Without any warning they would walk into my Davis office for a visit. One time he called me and said he was at the Sioux Falls airport and didn't have a car. Would I come and pick him up? I had just come into the house from working in the field so I told him I'd clean up and come to the airport.

On our way back home, the weather turned nasty. There were funnel clouds dancing all over the place and we were in the heart of a storm warning. We were about seven miles from our farm when it looked like we were driving right into a funnel cloud. I started backing up in hopes of avoiding it. In terms of size, it wasn't a massive funnel, but it was throwing dirt all over. It crossed the road right in front of us. Thankfully it missed us.

The next morning, Pastor John spoke at our church.

"If you know Harlan, you're aware that he never wants to be outdone in anything," Pastor John told the congregation. "He treated me to some real excitement yesterday on the way to his home. We nearly ran right into a tornado."

Pastor John made a special trip to South Dakota a few years ago. His health was failing, and he wanted one final visit. His son, Dirk, brought him. Numerous members of our congregation had the opportunity to spend time with him while he was here. Rita and I were blessed when Pastor John and Dirk insisted on treating us and sharing a meal with them at the Tea Steak House before they returned home. I'll always remember Pastor John as a Holy Spirit-filled, passionate person who loved God and loved people.

I've never allowed my wheelchair to keep me off the dance floor. There's just something about hearing the music start, a good fast song or country western favorite, and it's almost like I can't keep my wheelchair off the dance floor. It says, "Hey! We gotta' go!"

How do I dance in a wheelchair? These days dancing moves are pretty loose and sometimes crazy. People make up their own dance moves, which makes it easier for me to get out and enjoy dancing my way.

Before getting out on the floor, I used to elevate my wheelchair seat as high as it would go. I liked getting closer to my dance partner. Now my chair has a safety feature that keeps it from moving if the seat is up high, so I raise it as high as I can. I usually only dance to fast songs, slow dancing doesn't work as well.

When the music starts, I dance side to side or swing around my dance partner, do circles, etc. Rita isn't a dancer and I love to dance, so I take advantage of times when I can get out on the floor. If I have a good dance partner, they hold onto my hand, go back and forth and twirl around. There are a lot of ways to move my chair if I figure it out.

When we celebrated Loretta's 70th birthday (Rita's sister), we stayed at a hotel in Grand Rapids, Minnesota. Other members of Rita and Loretta's family stayed there, too.

The night we were there, a wedding reception was held in the hotel banquet room. As we were visiting, two of Rita's nieces dared me to go to the banquet room and get out on the floor to dance. I told them only if they would dance with me. They didn't think I would do it. They should have known better than to dare me.

Before I went to the banquet room, I wanted to know the bride's name. It would help me pull off my ruse. My plan was to say I was her Uncle Louie from Detroit.

I entered the banquet room and immediately bumped into the bride. I had my "Uncle Louie" Spiel all ready, but I couldn't keep a straight face while I said it. s

"Congratulations. We're very happy for you," I told her. She smiled very nicely but looked at me with a bit of a frown.

"Do I know you?" she asked. I couldn't lie.

"No, my family and I are staying here this weekend," I said. "I couldn't resist stopping in to watch people dance. I love to dance."

Long story short, I ended up dancing with the bride! My nieces, who were watching it all outside the banquet room door, came in and I danced with them, too. I've been the envy of those girls ever since.

One other adventure I will never forget (or repeat) was a visit to the Bethlehem Cave in the Black Hills. I wasn't crazy about entering the cave, but some friends graciously invited me to join them on their trip and talked me into it.

I didn't realize how claustrophobic I was until we got down into that cave. I had a manual wheelchair at the time and the cave wasn't handicapped accessible by any stretch of the imagination.

When we went in, it was just our guide, Dennis, Diane, and me. In one narrow passage of the cave both rims of the chair wheels scraped the side of the passage. I envisioned my chair becoming lodged between the narrow passage walls and never getting back out!

When we hit a plateau that was more open, I told Dennis and Diane I wasn't going to go any further into the cave. I would just sit right there and wait for them to return. Thankfully they didn't coerce me to continue. If they had, I would have become a screaming Mimi.

As I waited, their voices slowly faded into silence. I could hear the drip, drip, drip of moisture coming off the cave walls and other unfamiliar, unrecognizable sounds.

"What if something happens to them?" I thought. "What if they can't get back here again? No one else even knows I'm here!" All kinds of terrible thoughts raced through my mind during the 15 minutes or so I sat there.

I was never so thankful as when I finally heard their voices again. "Thank you, God!" I whispered. "Now get me out of here!"

I knew we'd have to return through that same narrow passage, but we made it through. It was never so good to see daylight when we reached the opening again. I knew I would never enter another cave.

One other time when I was with Dennis and Diane, we went to the Sioux Empire Fair. The midway featured a double Ferris Wheel. I was sure it would be fun to ride on it. There wasn't room for all three of us in a seat, so Diane and I sat together. I wasn't strapped in, but I rested my feet on the metal floor of the seat and braced myself against the bar across the front of the seat.

We were both enjoying the ride when the Ferris Wheel stopped with us on the very top. We must have set up there for at least five minutes. I couldn't help myself, I had to rock that seat back and forth for some excitement. Diane got excited, but not in a good way.

"Stop that!" she screamed at me.

"I'm just trying to make it more fun," I told her.

One thing on my bucket list was a hot air balloon ride. I knew a balloonist, Dwayne Waack, who was acquainted with my distant cousin. Dwayne lived near Sioux Falls. I asked him to put my name on a list to have a ride.

To make sure I could get into the balloon gondola (basket), I arranged to take a tethered ride, which didn't at all satisfy my curiosity about riding in a hot air balloon.

My distant cousin, Dorothy Overgaard, once shared with me that she, too, would like to take a hot air balloon ride. I suggested we do it together.

When she heard that my name was on Dwayne's list, she said, "I know that guy! I went to school with him in Kadoka." With that connection, it wasn't long before I received a call from Dwayne asking if I wanted to take my ride that same evening. It was a beautiful day.

Since Rita and I were already on our way to Sioux Falls we said we would be there to take the ride.

I called Dorothy to let her know of our plans. She was hesitant but agreed to go along, even on short notice. Her grandchildren were visiting, so I told her to just bring them and her husband along. Later she let me know how grateful she was that I "twisted her arm."

I had planned to use a sling I rigged up that would hold me up in my chair during the ride so I could see over the side of the balloon gondola. However, with the unexpected call, I wouldn't have that with me.

Our trip to Sioux Falls was to stop at Children's Care, where I get my wheelchairs, to take care of some wheelchair business. Staff member Pat Campbell had worked with my wheelchairs many times. I explained my balloon ride plan and asked if he might have anything that would help me sit tall in my chair during the ride. He assured me he would come up with something. He also told me he knew Dwayne, had worked with him as a balloonist in the past, and was instrumental in Dwayne's decision to become a balloonist.

"Would you like to go along on the ride?" I asked. He said he would love to.

Now that we had everyone lined up for the ride, we needed the "perfect" balloon-riding weather. The evening turned out to be a little too perfect. There was just no wind. Dwayne was apprehensive about taking the balloon up. But we had all these people waiting.

I assured Dwayne that I wasn't afraid to go up in the balloon, thanks to my daring, adventure-loving nature. I wasn't averse to "living on the edge."

"Be prepared for a bumpy landing," Dwayne said. "Sometimes the gondola slides when we come down."

Even though I knew that kind of landing wouldn't be the best for me, I really wanted a hot air balloon ride. So up we went!

The balloon was in the air for about 45 minutes. To my dismay, we only traveled three or four blocks during that time. The winds were just too calm. Imagine that, in South Dakota!

We were hovering over a well-to-do neighborhood when Dwayne decided it was time to bring the balloon down. It was a gentle landing, but not real flat terrain. The fun thing about coming down was seeing all the adults and kids in that neighborhood who came flooding out the houses, shouting "Hello!" and waving at us. They were excited!

Once we landed, Dwayne put a bit of air in the balloon so he and his helpers could "walk" it up to a flatter surface. I had no trouble getting out of the gondola there. I was disappointed that we weren't able to get out of town with the balloon, but I thought I could always get on Dwayne's list and try it all again.

My next experience was riding in a two-seat para-glider.

In 2010, through fellow church member Mark Eitrem, I learned about a group of ultralight trike glider owners who held an annual meet at the Vermillion airport. He invited me to come down and watch. "You might even get a ride," he said.

Of course, I took him up on the offer. It was there I met Larry Miller, a para-glider pilot. He knew I was interested in riding one of these machines, so he decided he and a crew of helpers would get me into the thing one way or another.

There's a lot of bars and framework on these machines, which complicated the process necessary to get me into the para-glider seat.

"I don't bend real easy," I warned them.

To get into that seat, I had to spread my legs apart more than what I was used to or what even was totally comfortable. But I decided I was going to take a ride even if it killed me. I teased Rita about having my insurance premium paid up.

"I definitely do," she said. "Someone here has to keep a level head."

I'm so glad I persisted in taking this ride. What an absolute rush it was to glide effortlessly across the sky. I wasn't at all frightened. I could see as far as Ponca, Nebraska, where my cousin Brenda Wortmann and her husband John live.

"Is there any place you want to go on the other side of the Missouri?" Larry asked. I directed him to the Wortmann's farm.

It took a bit to locate the farm. Everything looks different from that high vantage point. But we did find the ranch and circled it three different times. Unfortunately, they weren't home that day.

"Your cousin won't shoot at us when we're circling overhead, will he?" Larry thought our presence in the sky might alarm them.

"As long as they don't know I'm with you you're safe," I told Larry.

Even though we didn't get to see the Wortmanns, we spied a deer on the run and glided over the top of an irrigator that was running in an alfalfa field. Our ride lasted for about 45 minutes. It was much more exciting than I expected.

In 2011 Rita and I were invited to come back and ride again. Rita had declined the offer to ride the first year we attended the meet and Larry asked me if she would want to ride now.

"Absolutely not," I told him. "She will tell you no way." He asked her anyway and Rita made a liar out of me. She agreed to go for a short glide, too. I couldn't believe it.

I once heard that we have no choice in growing older, but we can choose whether we want to grow up. I don't ever plan to grow up if it means not enjoying new adventures and experiences. I will always want to know what's around the corner or over the hill.

Never underestimate the enthusiastic spirit of a small town.

One of our community's most well-known events is the Davis Winter Stock Production, an annual show that was first organized in 1983.

Charlie Larson first organized the show, which was the presentation of a play Charlie wrote. Local residents were featured in the play when it was presented in the Davis American Legion and Auxiliary building. That organization was always so gracious to allow us to use their building.

Supplies for the performances have been purchased locally, which helps support Davis businesses. From the beginning, any profits from the show have been donated to help meet the needs of local residents who have medical issues or other types of financial challenges. Other recipients of funds have included After Prom events and improvements on local buildings, such as the American Legion building. Since its inception, the shows have raised a total of $163,000 for the community.

The American Legion building barely accommodated the audiences who turned out for the first productions. I'm not sure how they ever fit everyone in. Initially, we built our own stage for the shows, which was taken down and stored afterward. When the American Legion expanded their building, we were able to leave the stage in place, which greatly reduced the amount of work needed to prepare for the production.

Rita and I were involved in the shows beginning in 1983. She continues as the organization's treasurer.

We've put on plays at numerous schools, including Hurley and Centerville. Our "claim to fame" with the shows happened in 1989, the year South Dakota turned 100. When one of our South Dakota Senators, Alice Kundert, heard about us, she contacted Charlie and said, "You've made a name for yourself. We would like to have you be part of our 100th year celebration at Mount Rushmore." That required transporting all our props and driving everyone and everything to Mount Rushmore. It was a lot of work but was also a great honor and fun.

As time went on, Rita and I found it more difficult to attend the

241

practices leading up to each presentation. It also became more challenging to memorize all our lines! Rita continued with the productions for a few years after I bowed out. Now we find it to be a great deal of fun to be on the audience-side of the curtain.

The play was postponed in 2020, due to Covid. However, because of Covid, they also added the option for anyone to watch the production on Zoom in 2021.

In recent years, this group has expanded their presentations to include dinner theaters and live-stream events. For a small town with less than 100 residents, this group has realized some great accomplishments.

When my cousin Sharon passed away, I was touched by the care giving she received through hospice. Sharon suffered from COPD and spent her last days in a nursing home. Her hospice volunteer brought a lot of comfort and provided wonderful care for her at the time.

That experience led me to contact the Sioux Falls AsaraCare hospice and volunteer my time. I completed their training program, learning about things I should or shouldn't say or do. For the most part, it's important for a visiting hospice volunteer to be sensitive to the patient and allow them to share as they desire. Remembering that the point of my calls/visits is about them and not me is helpful.

Once I completed the training, I looked forward to reaching out to people who were suffering in one way or another.

My first duty was to call bereaved families to see how they were doing and ask if they would like to have someone visit them. Some took advantage of the offer, others said they were doing okay and weren't in need of the hospice services.

Many times, the folks I called were thankful to be able to talk to someone about their loss and share their feelings. After volunteering for a time, I was invited to call on people who resided in the Lennox nursing home and were in the hospice program.

It was easy for me to oblige because Mom was still alive then and I was visiting her at the nursing home anyway. Eventually, I visited some people at the Centerville and Beresford nursing homes.

One part of this volunteer service that I enjoyed was hearing people talk about their fond memories of loved ones they had lost. Usually people talked about growing up with the person, their hobbies or occupation. At the close of our conversation I always read a scripture and prayed with them if they were willing to do that.

All the time I volunteered there was only one person that didn't want prayer. I was advised of that before I met with him. Even though this person didn't want to hear or talk about God, I did share how God has blessed me in so many ways throughout my life.

Because I'm comfortable with the thought about my own death, I found it easy enough to talk to others who were facing death. We know all of us will die one day. As long as we know Jesus we don't have to fear dying. There are caring hands we cannot see who will help us through the experience.

It's difficult to counsel or bring comfort to someone who is afraid to die. A few times I was asked if a hospice member could call me when death approached. I was always happy to say yes.

The most difficult hospice members I encountered were some who weren't able to talk due to a stroke. Sometimes they attempted to talk, but it was difficult to understand them. That's more challenging for a hospice volunteer. In those instances I sometimes played music. It could convey many things that couldn't be verbalized. I usually knew ahead of time what kind of music the patient enjoyed so I could find it on my phone before I visited.

Most of the time I spent between 15 and 30 minutes with hospice patients. I enjoyed volunteering for hospice about twice each month. During Covid, I did a Zoom visit with a hospice patient. It was great to see her face light up when we were able to talk. I think most times people are touched to realize that someone cares about them. I decided to give up volunteering late in 2020.

When a merging of hospice services occurred, the Hospice

243

Coordinator I worked with was no longer there. It seemed an appropriate time for me to make some changes, too.

We met Melissa Skaff through the Wolf Pack Special Olympics team. She was also a volunteer and we both helped with the Outdoor Track events. Before the events were held, volunteers gathered to practice and prepare. After one of the practices, Melissa and I decided to race from one end of the track to the other. Of course, I backed off and allowed her to win. Since that race Melissa and I bonded. She's a very positive, loving, and outgoing person. We both enjoy doing adventurous, "crazy" things. And she and I can talk about anything. She teaches children with special needs at the Junior High level.

Melissa has gone kayaking with me several times at the Sioux Falls Family Park and Covell Lake. The evening event at Covell Lake is the final kayaking event there for each year. With the help of the Sioux Falls fire department, hot dogs and other treats are served.

Melissa Skaff is like an adopted niece to me and Rita. Not only has she taken me kayaking several times, she has accompanied us on some trips, shared some exciting adventures with us, and been a great help with my personal care.

The Sanford Accessible Wellness and Adaptive Sports Program provides everything someone like me needs to go out in a kayak, including an air bag under my knees so my knees are bent just a little and I stay comfortable during the ride.

Kayak's are very stable, balanced with downriggers, so they are unlikely to tip over in the water. That makes them a good option for folks like me to get out on the water.

At the Family Park, there's a limited area where kayakers are supposed to go. So guess who went beyond those boundaries? Melissa and I didn't go very far past the boundary. But it didn't take long for park officials to catch up to us and guide us back to the approved area.

Melissa also accompanied Rita and me on a trip to Spearfish for the South Dakota Special Olympics State meet. Melissa served as my main caretaker on that trip and she talked me into trying a hot tub for the first time.

Along the way to Spearfish we stopped at South Dakota's Badlands. It was windy and cold the day we stopped and we were all inside the van, taking in as much of the beauty as we could. There was a winding path that looked so inviting, but it was too cold for me to be out on it.

"Melissa, would you go around the corner along that path and see what's there? Will you take some pictures there?" She graciously agreed to my request. When she came back she said, "Unc, you have to come out and see this." She and Rita bundled me up and Melissa refused to take no for an answer. She was right. It was an amazingly beautiful sight.

Not only is Melissa daring, crazy, and courageous. She is also very caring and is rewarded when she sees others enjoy life.

On another trip to Spearfish, Melissa was with Rita and me when we went to Wyoming's Devils Tower. It was amazing to watch people scaling that unexplained phenomenon.

There's a path that goes up and around Devil's Tower. Of course, the sign there says the path doesn't accommodate wheelchairs. Melissa looked at me and said, "You are going to do it, aren't you?"

I looked at her and we headed up the path. It was narrow, but I had no trouble navigating it. Some of the sights from that elevation were astounding. We didn't have time to go all the way to its end, and we expected at any minute we might hear from Rita and the others waiting in the area below, telling us to come down. The view from there was beautiful.

I am forever grateful for Melissa's outgoing, adventurous nature and her willingness over the years to share some very fun times with me and Rita.

A few years ago, Melissa joined Rita and me on a 10-day trip to visit Ardie and her family in Michigan. Both Melissa and I were looking forward to visiting the beach at Holland State Park. It's one of the most beautiful beaches in the area.

Melissa helped with the 750-mile drive. She also helped with my care.

Ardie's daughter Shelley was able to join us on the beach part of the time, when she wasn't at her job. Both these girls love a good time. About seven out of those 10 days we were on the beach. Ardie and Rita enjoyed some other types of activities, and Rita had time to relax and enjoy reading on Ardie's deck.

Shelley took me and Melissa to some different parks and along some beautiful trails while we were there. But the beach that year was the best.

In Holland State Park they have portable walkways that take visitors just about to the water. That was really helpful because, off the walkway, my chair quickly bogged down in the sand. People were very friendly and helpful if I did get stuck.

When we found a gentleman who was drinking beer at the beachhouse concession stand, he advised us that we couldn't drink beer on the beach. We had to consume it right there at the concession stand. We visited with him while we all enjoyed a beer. That day I had my cup holder on the wheelchair and after we were near the water for a while, this guy came up and poured a beer into my and Melissa's cup. We thought that gesture was pretty cool.

Melissa made sure I got to feel what it was like to get my feet in the sand. She set me on the edge of the sidewalk and poured sand over my feet. It felt like sugar instead of sand.

On a day when Shelley was with us, I bought a lounging chair I found at a store. The girls parked it right by the edge of the water and set me in it so I could experience the sensation of water splashing over my feet and legs. It was so impressive to see how helpful people were to carry me from my wheelchair to the lounging chair. They thought it was neat the girls gave me this experience. The first time we had help it was a couple of ladies. The next time it was two guys.

It was Saturday now. The days were slipping by. Melissa texted me, even though we were in the same room. "Unc, are you ready to go to the beach?" I texted back, "Yes, I certainly am."

Ardie advised us that we might not be able to find a parking spot on a Saturday. Still, Melissa and I wanted to try.

When we arrived at the beach, it was swamped. It looked like we wouldn't find a parking spot. As we drove into the parking lot a car started backing out. That was a God thing! We drove into that spot. When we got to the beach we took some selfies and sent them back to Ardie and Rita. "Wanted you to know we made it!"

It was just an affirmation to me that, even if a dream sounds crazy, you have to try. When you find others who are as adventurous as you, people like Melissa Skaff, they may help you fulfill your dreams. Melissa certainly did that for me. We call her our adopted niece.

My adopted niece, Melissa Skaff, treated me to the opportunity to feel the sensation of sand on my feet on the beach at Holland State Park. I loved it!

Rita and Harlan with friends Mason, Kate, and Paxton Schramm, enjoying Falls Park at Sioux Falls.

*"And my God will
supply all your
needs according to
His riches in glory
in Christ Jesus."*

PHILIPPIANS 4:19

SIXTEEN

POWERING UP

As a kid, I never had a wheelchair until I came to CCHS. Prior to that, Mom and Dad had a buggy they used when we were away from home. It folded up so they could carry it in the trunk. It was good sized and we used it for several years.

My Aunt's father, Bert Poppinga made a wooden frame that was almost like parallel bars. I used it outside so I could stand up sometimes.

Around the farm I learned to get around in a coaster wagon. Opa came up with the idea of putting a backrest in the wagon so I could sit up and be more comfortable as I was moving around the yard.

While the manual wheelchair I had at CCHS was helpful, my mobility really improved when I acquired my power chair. This chair had all kinds of different functions. I could stretch out my legs, tilt myself back and raise the seat up to sit at a table or desk. It was great to have the ability to shift into different positions while I sat in the chair.

But let me back up a bit. The Sioux Falls Children's Care Rehabilitation Center (CCRC) wanted to evaluate me in order to custom fit a wheelchair for me. The therapists I worked with were Libby Gardner and Mark Nelson. They started with measuring my hip movement to see how far I could lean forward. They needed to know if I could sit at a 90-degree angle. I was pretty young at the time and hesitant to comply with their directions.

Libby was sitting on a cot and wanted me to sit between her legs, using them like the arms of a chair. Libby wasn't put off by my tension. She had the gift of pulling the tension out of a person and carefully worked with me until I was able to fully relax and sit back against her arms.

One thing I wanted in a wheelchair was some speed and some power. I tried out several different models but wasn't finding quite what I had in mind.

Several people worked to help make splints for my wrists so I could bend them up. Linda Bomhuff was one very good therapist who assisted with making cast splints.

I stopped in to try chairs a number of times, but none of them quite met my needs. Mark called one day saying that they might have found the chair that would suit me.

When I went to the rehab center to try it out, Mark got down on the floor behind the chair.

"Let's see if you can drag me across the floor with this chair," he said. He weighed about 240 pounds, and I drug him across the carpeted floor without any problem.

"Now take the chair out into the parking lot," he told me. There was a lot of snow in the lot and it was warm enough that day the snow was sloppy from melting. I voiced my concerns about getting the chair dirty and/or stuck in the snow.

"This thing is supposed to jump curbs, so let's see if it really does," the guy told me.

"What if I wreck the chair?"

"It's a demo so don't worry about that."

The building was right on 41st Street in Sioux Falls, a street where the traffic almost never stops. Here I am running through the snow in that parking lot to see if I can get this chair stuck in a snowbank.

252

As people drove by they must have been wondering about the wild guy plowing into snow piles. They probably thought I had more problems than just needing a wheelchair to get around.

I did get stuck in the snow but didn't ruin the chair. It turned out to be just the model with all the features I needed. I thought maybe it almost had too many features. I wasn't certain I would really need to adjust the height of the seat very often. However, Mark said, "Harlan. Go for it. If Medicare says no, it's no. But at least try it." He was right. Medicare approved the chair without any problems and I often use that feature.

Having this powerful wheelchair, a Permobil brand, I wanted to see if the cheater wheels in the back would hold me from going over backwards while I went through a ditch. Niece Shelley was behind me in case the cheater wheels didn't keep me from tipping. It was kind of like playing Evel Knievel.

It definitely took some speed to come up out of the ditch. The front wheels of the chair came up off the ground, but the chair didn't tip over. Dad was standing close by watching my shenanigans.

"Do you think that's a smart thing to do?" he asked. "Please don't do that again. Do you have to push everything to the limit?"

Dad was probably right. I was known for occasional zany behavior, like going out in a heavy rain with Shelley. We both thought it would be neat to put on a bathing suit and go outside in the warm rain. Of course, we wouldn't have gone out in a storm.

When it was time for a new wheelchair, I was working with Jill, an occupational therapist. It was beginning to be difficult to get repair parts for the old power chair I had (be sure to call them power chairs, not electric chairs), so it was time to upgrade. I was pretty certain that I wanted a chair that was very similar to my other one and I wanted a Permobil chair.

When I talked to Jill about the features I wanted in the new chair, she asked me about the possibility of getting a mid-drive chair instead of the rear wheel drive I'd been using. I told Jill I didn't think I wanted a mid-drive.

However, when Jill ordered the demo chairs, she requested that the sales rep bring both types of chairs. When I went in to try the chairs, Jill encouraged me to at least try out the mid-drive.

"See what this chair will do in the snow," she said.

There I was, out in the parking lot again. I wanted to check this chair out, too. So I plunged into some snow that was deep enough to come up to my knees. The chair wasn't powerful enough to get me out of that snowbank. I had it so stuck that it almost took a tow truck to get me out. When Jill and another OT, Arlen Klamm, finally got me out they asked if I was having fun yet.

"Oh, yes," I said.

"We want you to take this chair into that store over there and go up and down some aisles," Jill told me. "That will help you see how maneuverable this chair can be."

I followed her instructions and boy was I happy with the results! Jill was absolutely right about the value of a mid-drive in a wheelchair. It's so much easier to turn and move the chair in tight spaces. It warmed my heart to know that she took the initiative to give me a chance to try this kind of chair. I've never looked back.

One other feature of my recent wheelchairs has been color. How great to have the option to choose a favorite color. Even though I'm a Minnesota Vikings fan, I am not influenced by their colors, I just like the color purple. The last two wheelchairs I've acquired have been purple.

The most recent wheelchairs have more safety functions than ever. Features such as if the chair is raised too high it won't move because it may be too top heavy and tip over. Most of the time it's not an issue, but there are times when I'd like to raise my chair a little higher to be on a level with other people, and be able to move around, too.

Having a power wheelchair gives me so much more independence. I can adjust my position without having someone help me. In addition to a seatbelt, I also have a kneepad to hold me in the chair better, especially over rough ground.

Another nice thing about these modern wheelchairs is my

ability to stay in the chair when I go to the dentist. That's about the only time I use the headrest on my chair. I can also stay in the chair most of the time when I go to doctor appointments. It's so nice not to have to get out of the chair and lay on an exam table, especially since the curvature of my spine makes laying on a hard table very uncomfortable.

When a person spends 16 to 18 hours sitting in a chair every day, that chair needs to fit the person rather than having the person fit the chair.

I like it that my chair is fitted with one bracket that holds my guns, a cup holder, and a table, which is very handy if I'm someplace where I can't get up to the table.

The newest outdoor wheelchairs are on tracks, which allows users to go over rough terrain and have mobility in muddy or snowy conditions.

The process for creating a chair for a specific person's needs now involves sitting in a sandbag type of chair that sucks out all the air around my body. It produces a three-dimensional shape, which accommodates the curvature of my spine.

My current wheelchair allows me to do things like tilt back so I can stretch my legs. I can drop the foot pedals down to help take pressure off my feet. If I lean back too far or raise up in the chair, it won't move. That's a safety feature that helps keep it from tipping. I know it's helpful, but to me it's very annoying.

I've always made sure my gun bracket fits my new chair. I couldn't hunt without it.

Every time I purchase a new chair, it requires some modifications. I'm thankful for this pit crew who take care of that for me: Pat Campbell, Mark Dahm, Arlen Klamm, Art Diaz, and Chris Rokeh.

Me with some of the rehab personnel (left to right): Art, Arlen, Mark, and Jill.

Me and Jill Barron, OT, with a new wheelchair.

"Give, and it will be given to you. A good measure, pressed down, shaken together and running over, will be poured into your lap. For with the measure you use, it will be measured unto you."

LUKE 6:38

SEVENTEEN

MY TURN TO GIVE BACK

O ften, one of the symptoms of cerebral palsy is tightness and contracture of limb muscles. It's something I've experienced more and more over the years. The muscles in my hands have caused my fingers to curl under more and more, making it very challenging if not impossible to do many things.

In a heated pool, the water creates a soothing, buoyant environment that allows my muscles to relax. It also gives me the ability to move my legs to a degree and release some of the muscle stress.

I started warm water therapy a number of years ago with a physical therapist, Lois Vogel. In addition to helping me get into a warm pool, Lois developed a stretching routine which was very helpful in relieving muscle tightness in my arms and legs. She provided the same types of therapy for residents at CCHS.

When Lois left that position, Carole Wolf, who was working with CCHS residents, offered to learn the routine Lois had organized and continue my exercise. I was happy to accept that offer.

Eventually, Carole took a position at Sanford Aquatics in Sioux Falls. She let me know that, if I wanted to do my exercises there, she was willing to continue doing it for me. I so enjoyed that warm water that I was happy to make the move with her.

In the past, warm water therapy helped me move my legs in the water, reduce overall muscle tension, and enjoy some time out of my wheelchair. These exercise sessions also opened an entirely new network of friends and wonderful life experiences for both me and Rita. Pictured here are Carole Wolf and niece Shelley working with me in the pool.

Throughout my life it has always intrigued me how God connects people and how a connection with one person can lead to connections with a new person and sometimes an entire new network of relationships. I am fascinated by that.

It was through my water exercises that I met Andrew Saugstad. He was one of the special needs children that Carole Wolf was helping with swimming lessons.

I was always impressed with how Carole could work with kids with special needs, who sometimes came to swimming lessons screaming, hollering, and very distraught. Carole had a way of helping them calm down and focus on their lesson. If a child was afraid of the water, it would only take a few sessions before Carole had them jumping into and enjoying the swimming pool.

Of course, some of the kids got a kick out of seeing me doing water exercises, too. Some of them started calling me "Grandpa."

At one of my water exercise sessions, Carole was working with Andrew Saugstad. Whenever Carole moved from working with Andrew, she directed him to keep an eye on me.

"If Harlan starts to drift, let me know," Carole instructed Andrew. The responsibility this gave Andrew was very beneficial for him. And somehow, Andrew and I connected almost right away. We easily "picked up" on one another. Before long, Andrew and I became good friends. As we became acquainted with his family, Jeanette and Clifton (his mother is a nursing instructor), they visited and sometimes offered to help us around the farm with different chores. Clifton grew up on the farm and still has farming in his blood.

Andrew is very affectionate. If we all go out to eat, Andrew wants to ride in our van. Now about 25 years old, Andrew has a unique ability to zero in on different things. He's very interested in and knowledgeable about wheels. One time when we met them at a restaurant, before we even said hello, Andrew piped up: "You have new tires on your wheelchair." It always touches me that Andrew has been the connection between us and his family, who have been a blessing in our lives.

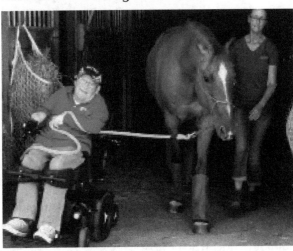

Rita and I grew close to Andrew Saugstad and his family. One day I had the pleasure of leading a horse back to its stall after Andrew finished a riding therapy session.

It seems we can share just about anything with Andrew's family.

As a medical person, Jeanette is comfortable with discussing my physical challenges and changes. She, Clifton, and I have been able to have some in-depth spiritual talks about many topics, which I so appreciate.

I'm a "want-to-know" kind of person and I've had some good talks with Jeanette about how my spinal curvature is affecting and will continue to affect my health.

Although we know that every part of our lives is in God's hands, the continued progression of the curvature of my spine will ultimately affect my lungs and heart. Because of her medical expertise, Jeanette recognizes physical changes in me more quickly than I do. In recent months she tells me she feels I'm entering my end-of-life journey.

Not everyone would be so open about these things, but I'm okay with that. I would rather know than just wonder.

I continually see changes in my body and that there are things I used to do that are more difficult or I can't do now. In a crazy way it's somewhat comforting to know that I'm closer to my end-of-life journey. I don't have a death wish, but I do have a heaven wish.

I am confident that I will go to heaven when I leave this world and the prospect of being released from this confining body is something I look forward to.

Carole was and still is the leader of the South Dakota United Wolf Pack Special Olympics team. As Carole and I became more acquainted, she suggested that Rita and I consider becoming Special Olympics volunteers. Rita assisted with signing in participants during practice and meets as well as helping with record keeping and fund raising.

"I believe you would be a valuable coach for these kids," Carole told me. "You certainly have the ability to inspire and motivate them."

One thing led to another, and the first thing I knew, Rita and I were volunteering for these special kids, and I completed training to be a coach for their Field and Track events.

As a coach, I encouraged young team members when they took

part in activities like throwing a ball. Just comments like, "Throw the ball as hard as you can!" "Run as fast as you can!" meant a great deal to these special athletes. I also helped them stay focused during the event.

If a youngster had just joined Special Olympics, my job as coach was to go ahead of them on the track and help them get the hang of running in a race or using their wheelchair to race and the importance of staying in their lane. As some of the athletes got older, they greatly enjoyed running past me as I raced down the track with them.

One young lady with CP was totally blind and didn't have much strength in one arm and hand. This little gal was pretty active. She used a walker and a wheelchair to get around.

She was training in a wheelchair race, and I was talking to her, helping guide her along the track since she couldn't see. It was great to see her determination and persistence. I applauded her just for her desire to compete.

What I forgot, when I was moving backwards so she could hear me better and I could keep my eyes on her, was that my left and right were now opposite to hers. One time I gave her wrong directions and ran her into a wall. Of course, I had to slip and do the same thing a couple more times. She let me know how she felt about that. "Harlan! Stop that!"

Rita and I have traveled with the Wolf Pack team to area meets in Brandon, Lennox, and to the State meets in Brookings, Spearfish, and Vermillion.

Carole also encouraged me to become a coach for the Special Olympics Bowling Team. As a coach, I was able to bowl, too. I learned many things about bowling from these young people.

The bowling alley, Empire Bowl in Sioux Falls, gave all of us a free ball and bag, which was pretty generous on their part. Like a number of the other team members, I place the bowling ball on a rail and give it a shove to send it down the alleyway.

One reason Carole asked me to help with the bowling activities was the fact that I needed help to bowl. These young Special

Olympics team members helped me to place my ball on the rail and helped me learn more about bowling in general. That opportunity gave those young people a chance to receive the reward that comes from helping others. Instead of always receiving help, now they were able to provide help to someone else.

Sometimes these young kids were reluctant to be my helper. When they got tired, they wanted to quit before we were all done. "Sorry," I told them. "This is part of our practice. It has to be done."

"Really?" they'd ask

"Yes, really. You don't want me to have to talk to Carole, do you?" Fortunately, I was always able to talk them through the situation. Not only have Rita and I enjoyed volunteering for Special Olympics, we connected with an entirely new "family" of people with whom we continue to enjoy working, sharing meals and visiting.

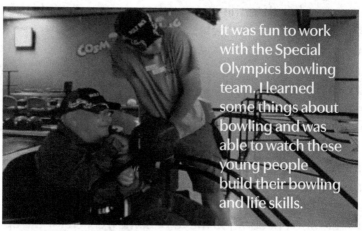

It was fun to work with the Special Olympics bowling team. I learned some things about bowling and was able to watch these young people build their bowling and life skills.

For some time, I had considered the possibility of becoming a body donor to The University of South Dakota (USD). But I'm a "want-to-know" kind of guy, and I was curious about what would happen to my body if I did donate it.

That prompted me to call USD and ask if I could tour the USD anatomy lab before I made my final decision as a body donor. They were happy to oblige.

The first time I toured the lab, my niece Shelley Young came with me. There were no medical students working there that day. No dissecting activities were underway. I liked what I saw, but I was still thinking on my decision.

In 2001, then Dean Paul Bliss (now deceased) gave me a tour and explained the donor program to me. He was a very colorful and interesting person and gave me an excellent tour. He made me feel very comfortable while I was there and answered all my questions. He greatly influenced my decision. About a week after the tour, I signed the papers and in 2012 became a body donor to USD.

When I was invited to speak to the med students, I was also invited to tour the lab again, while the students were there. My adopted niece Melissa Flannery accompanied me. She had just completed her Registered Nursing Degree and she was curious about the donor program, too. On that visit I met the Anatomy Department Head, Jane Gavin. She was a well-respected instructor. I'll always remember how comfortable she made us feel. She encouraged me to ask students questions and helped me don a white lab coat, so I was just like all the students in the lab!

USD professors and anatomy lab students

Before I left that day, Jane asked me if I would consider coming back again to speak to an anatomy class. I assured her I was no speaker.

"Don't worry. You won't be graded on your talk," she told me. "I encourage you to prepare something from your heart. I think new students will greatly benefit from what you share."

When the time came for me to speak, I had put a speech together. About 150 medical students gathered to hear my presentation. My niece Shelley was with me and I felt more comfortable.

The first time Dr. Jane Gavin invited me to speak to USD
med students, I was pretty nervous. In spite of my jitters,
it all went very well each time I was invited to talk.

At the close of that speech, I was again invited to tour the anatomy lab while students were dissecting bodies. I donned the necessary gown and observed several different tables where students were working. They were so gracious to answer my questions and allow me to get in close enough to see what they were doing. One thing that stood out to me was the size of the human voice box. It's tiny! I never expected so much noise to come out of something so small. I noticed that day that one table in the lab was different from the others.

"I wondered if you'd notice that," Jane said. "There's one here that's open underneath, designed to allow for someone in a wheelchair or stool to fit the chair underneath the table."

I thought about that for a moment. "Could I use that table when it's time for me to be dissected?" I think my question caught her off guard. She laughed.

"I guess that would be pretty appropriate, wouldn't it?" she said. So, in my file at USD, there's a note saying that is the table my body will be placed on.

So someday my body will be an instructor. And I certainly see God in all of this. It's a way I can give back something for his many blessings. Every person is different than everyone else ever born. Just the idea that our fingerprints are all unique is incredible. And students at USD will have an opportunity to find out what has made me different from others.

During a total of four visits to the anatomy lab, many students have commented on the fact that having an unusual body like mine, with CP, severe curvature of the spine, and other issues, will give them an added dimension to learn. They say that no pictures in books or plastic models can speak as clearly as an actual body.

Ms. Gavin has now moved to Atlanta, where she continues to teach on-line. I will always appreciate her kindness and accommodation of my request. The new director, Stewart Ingalls, also invited me to speak and again gave me opportunities to tour the anatomy lab.

As we walked through the lab, he pointed out some things of interest and allowed me to hold a heart. He pointed out that the enlarged liver of one body indicated that the person had liver cancer. Students were also very helpful and accommodating whenever I visited the lab.

About the same time these anatomy lab visits were happening, Occupational Therapy Instructor Dr. Barb Brockevelt and Dan Robbins came across an article that Mary Hurd had written about me. The story was about my membership in Breaking New Ground. This organization was formed in 1979 through the Purdue University Department of Agricultural and Biological Engineering's Breaking New Ground Resource Center. It has since served as a primary source for information and resources on rehabilitation technology for disabled persons working in agriculture.

This group gathered annually at different locations to share with others how they had modified equipment and tools so they can use them. I shared the designs that have been developed for me and contributed to a publication that contains the input of other Breaking New Ground members. Mary Hurd's article explained how this group operated and let people know that anyone who wanted to visit our farm to see these innovations was welcome.

After reading the article, the OT Department believed that Occupational Therapy (OT) students may be able to learn things from Rita and me that would help them in their careers. A hands-on visit would allow us to show them some of the everyday ways we function. By coming to the farm, the students could sit in my wheelchair, sit in the sling that lifted me out of my wheelchair and onto the lawn mower, and see the many modifications and adaptations that made it possible for me to mow the lawn, drive a tractor, etc.

Allison Naber was in the first group of USD students who visited our farm. Allison (seated on the lift) went on to become Dr. Naber and brought other OT students out for a visit.

In our first interaction with the USD OT students, eight students and their instructors, Carol Dodson and Jennifer Sorum, came to our farm. From that first visit it was such fun to have them at the farm that we wanted to continue hosting this fun outing.

One student in that first group was Allison Naber, who became Dr. Naber and an OT instructor. In later years she brought students to the farm.

Stacy Smallfield, pictured here with me in my tractor, was one of the OT instructors who brought OT students to the farm. We became great friends with her and her family.

Over the 17 years that we hosted OT students, it was fun to watch them as they learned more about what it's like to always be lifted out of my wheelchair when I want to do something on the farm. They also learned things like the fact that a zero-turn lawn mower was the only model I could operate. Some students quickly caught on to how to use things like the sling and the mower modifications on our John Deere Gator.

One year, when Stacy Smallfield was unable to attend our gathering, she requested that I serve as the instructor for the day. It was a new challenge for me, but since I was familiar with the

269

Among the hands-on experiences OT students gained by visiting us at the farm were the opportunity to see what it felt like to sit in a wheelchair, use modifications to operate our JD Gator, and be lifted out of the wheelchair onto the lawn mower.

As I've had to upgrade my wheelchairs, I've acquired several power wheelchairs, which made it possible for the OT students to experience what it's like to use a chair for mobility. And of course, we had to add some fun to the day. There were enough wheelchairs for several of us to have wheelchair races! In most cases I made sure I had the fastest chair, which caused some students to call me out, saying I was cheating. All in all, it was always fun to have the students at our home and I know they learned important details about what it's like to be disabled.

It didn't take long before we had between 26 and 28 students visiting us. Once the group was that large, we needed to split the students into two groups so each of them had time for hands-on experience. The students brought everything for the lunch, which was like a potluck, except the barbecue that Rita made. The morning group stayed long enough to enjoy lunch with the afternoon group.

One of the highlights of our summers were the visits from the OT classes. Seeing these young professionals hands-on experience with physical disability and knowing they wanted to learn and understand so they could help others was very rewarding.

I'll always remember the fishing trip we shared with the OT students at Yankton's Riverside Park when Stacy Smallfield was their instructor. One student and I decided to fish off a ramp on the west edge of the park. The dock had no railing, and the student was a bit apprehensive about having me go down onto it in my wheelchair. I guess it was possible that my wheelchair could keep going right off the dock.

However, I wasn't at all worried about fishing on that dock. One of the students yelled back to Rita, "Can I let him do this?" Rita's response was immediate.

"I don't think we can stop him," she yelled back. "If something happens, try to save the chair!"

This thank you note is one indication to us that the OT students we hosted were positively impacted by what they learned during their visit.

After a number of summer visits, I was invited by the OT faculty to be the keynote speaker at a hooding ceremony. I was humbled and honored by their request. I was also somewhat intimidated by the thought that the audience for this event would be parents and relatives of the students, but I agreed to prepare a speech. I asked Stacy to be on stage with me to turn pages for me if I needed help.

We had become good friends with Stacy and her family (who have now moved to St. Louis), so she graciously sat right beside me while I gave my talk.

"If I faint, will you just push me aside and finish my talk?" She agreed! What a privilege and honor it was to fulfill this request, even

272

though I had lots of butterflies in my stomach. I was honored with the opportunity to speak at three different OT student hooding ceremonies. It was extra special to me that for two of the three times the students requested that I come and speak. Never in my wildest imagination did I ever think I would find myself giving a keynote speech at an Occupational Therapy Hooding ceremony.

For the last two talks, I used a digital device so I could just scroll through my speech notes. I guess no one could tell how nervous I was because they gave me a standing ovation when I was done and many compliments afterward.

I know I came through all those events with God's help and much prayer. Each time I went it was exciting, but it never got easier. My nerves were still somewhat jangled.

One group of USD OT graduates.

Around 2012 Rita and I started a small scholarship fund for the OT students. One way the scholarship is funded is through a 5K run/walk/roll. For the first eight years, we held the 5K at Vermillion.

My fastest time with the run/walk/roll when I went by myself was 43 minutes, 4 seconds. That speed wasn't really good for my back since I hit a couple of bumps along the way. Good thing I had my seatbelt on.

During the 2018 5K, USD OT student Becca Gaikowski hitched a ride on the back of my chair as we made our way up a hill along the run/walk/roll route.

One year at the 5K, four of us decided to go at a leisurely pace, not caring about our time. In Vermillion, the event route included a hill. If I heard students complaining during the race, I had to kid them by saying, "The hill certainly hasn't bothered me yet!"

Becca couldn't resist the opportunity to tease me back.

"Can I jump on the back of your chair, Harlan? I'm running out of energy," she said.

"Heck, yes," I told her. She jumped on the chair and rode with me as we finished climbing the hill. The other three students with us gave her a bad time about "wimping out" on the hill. Just another fun adventure!

A delicious brunch follows each 5K, giving an opportunity to do some visiting and connecting with other participants. Prizes are given out, too.

In 2020, with Covid restrictions, Emily Heumiller set up a virtual 5K, which was successful. Over Friday, Saturday, and Sunday participants could select their time and place to do the walk/run/roll. Time keeping and submission were on the honor system.

Emily and I completed our race together in Sioux Falls along the bike trail. We ended up doing a double 5K by the time we were finished. It took us a little over three hours to complete a leisurely walk along our route.

Starting of the 8th annual 2019 5k Race at Prentis Park in Vermillion.

We have had so much fun with these USD students. It wasn't long before it became clear we had no choice but to become a "Yote," as they pulled us into their camp. Yes, we did catch some flack from our South Dakota State University (SDSU) friends.

That first time I went to a USD girls' basketball game the new athletic complex was about a year old, if that. I mentioned to Becca that it would be fun to go to a game in the new complex, but I wasn't sure there would be a place for me to park my wheelchair. Since Becca and Angie Kaiser had never been there either, they didn't have an answer. They promised to check it out and asked one of their professors, Dr. Bob Brockevelt. Within a couple of days, Dr. Brockevelet had obtained three tickets and had everything arranged for us. Becca and Angie let me know that everything was all set.

They picked me up at the farm and drove our van so Rita could have a respite day. When we got to the campus, Becca and Angie showed me some of the new classrooms, then we went to the athletic complex. We went to a good-sized room where there was coffee, goodies, and beer.

"Where are we?" I asked.

"We received tickets for the VIP section!" Becca and Angie had been keeping the secret about the free VIP tickets for several days. The girls were just as excited as I was since none of us had ever been in the VIP section. We were able to watch the game through a window or go out onto the VIP section deck, which is where we went to enjoy the game. Every once in a while, a student came along to ask if we needed anything. We all had a great time.

The following year I was able to obtain free VIP tickets and surprise Mallory Paitz and Jessica Reishus who went to a game with me. Now, whenever Rita and I go to a game, we sit on the top deck. There's really no poor seating for a wheelchair in the entire complex. And the family restrooms are very accessible and accommodating for handicapped folks.

Angie (left) and Becca (right) and I were surprised with free VIP tickets to the USD girls' basketball game.

One year Rita and I surprised Jessica Reishus (left) and Mallary Paitz with VIP tickets for a USD game.

How great it was to capture a photo with the University of South Dakota mascot, Charlie the Coyote!

It was 2019 when Rita and I recognized the need to "pass the torch" for OT students visiting the farm. We spoke with Dr. Naber about the need to find a new location. It was getting to be a lot of work for Rita and I to get all the equipment ready and host the students. Dr. Naber was very understanding and surprised us with the news that another volunteer had already agreed to host the event when Rita and I were ready.

"For the past couple of years, we had a volunteer who offered to host us at their farm," she told us. Turned out that farmer and his wife were our good friends Rick and Mary Hurd. Rick has always been one of my heroes. Rick was 17 when he had a virus that nearly took his life and left him paralyzed. He never allowed his limitations to hold him back. He worked for four or five different companies,

278

selling augers, haying equipment, grain handling equipment, etc. He also has a modified van so he can get in and out of it by himself.

What an honor and pleasure to hand off this fun activity to such giving and kind people, someone Rita and I highly regard.

The first year the students visited the Hurd farm, Rita and I had the opportunity to join them. We will always remember fondly the times we shared with these young professionals and appreciate the ongoing friendships with some of the students and USD faculty. Over the years we have maintained a friendship with a number of these students.

From the comments and all the fun we had with the OT students, I know our relationship with them was beneficial. I hope they know, too, that we gained so much pleasure and reward from hosting them and sharing insights that may help them throughout their career. It was truly a win-win relationship.

I love working with young people because they're so full of life and are full of life. Their tendency to maintain a positive outlook helps me remain young at heart.

Rita and I along with Drs. Barb and Bob Brockevelt and Allison Naber at a USD Game.

Each year that OT students came to the farm it was customary to take a group photo as we gathered around my John Deere tractor. This is one of the groups we hosted.

Starting of the 2017 5K race at Prentis Park in Vermillion.

For our 2021 5K, Katy Foster served as the event's head organizer.

Starting our 10th Annual 5K Race in 2021
at Vermillion's Prentis Park.

"My flesh and my heart may fail, but God is the strength of my heart and my portion forever."

PSALM 73:26

EIGHTEEN

Visions Of Sunset

You may be wondering what prompted me to write this book about my life, sharing what I've experienced and achieved. Certainly, everyone has a valuable life-story.

While many factors for my motivation come to mind, one of my top priorities has been to encourage everyone I know – those who have also experienced physical limitations and those who have been blessed with physical agility – to never stop dreaming and not allow obstacles to keep them from pursuing those dreams. I've stated many times that I am a "need to know" kind of person. I cannot imagine being restricted from asking questions and/or enjoying new experiences. Even though some of my "adventures" may not have been very prudent.

As a youngster, I was blessed to have parents who never told me, "You can't do that. You're handicapped." Their efforts to help me live my life to the fullest made all the difference in how I saw myself. It also gave me the confidence I needed to pursue the interests and passions God placed in my heart.

It brings me great joy to share with others what an incredible blessing my wife, parents, sisters, and extended family have been and continue to be throughout my life. Commitment and faithfulness to God and to each other has and continues to serve all of us well.

And who has been blessed with more kind and creative friends than I have? You've met many of them through these chapters, but there's an endless list of those who have done all they could – in small or big ways – to help me along my life journey.

My desire to describe my life experiences was fueled by the speaking opportunities I was given by the University of South Dakota Occupational Therapy students and Professors. How wonderful it has been to play a role in the development of these enthusiastic and talented young therapy students. My time on earth is limited, but hopefully what I've contributed to their understanding of the people they will encounter in their careers will live on. My family certainly lived out the idea that giving to and helping others is key to living a joyful life. It will please me to know that part of my life's legacy will reflect that same perspective.

As for the time limits on my life, it's clear that my strength is waning, which is typical of most people as they reach an advanced age. I'm also experiencing the effects of my curved spine, another result of cerebral palsy. As with anyone with spinal curvature, as the condition advances, I'm experiencing increased discomfort in both sitting and moving around. I feel more and more pressure on my internal organs – heart, lungs, etc. Some days I experience dizzy spells and have also had a few mental lapses when brain fog settled in and hindered my conversation or thought process.

Throughout the years I've met and befriended numerous medical personnel. I appreciate their willingness to be open and honest with me about the reality of my physical condition. Losing strength in my legs means I'm more confined to my wheelchair. It's more difficult to bathe and take care of simple daily activities.

What flexibility I did have in my arms and hands has also declined. I can still do some writing, but it's even hard for me to decipher what I've scribbled down. Every muscle in my body becomes less and less flexible despite my weekly therapy sessions with Brian Iverson. If I feel tense at all, it just makes all the muscles

284

that much less flexible.

One of our good friends, an instructor of nursing, is comfortable in discussing with me the likely path that lies ahead of me in terms of physical decline. Restriction of my lungs and heart puts serious stress on every other part of my body. It's actually comforting to me to be able to acknowledge the specter of a heart attack, stroke, pneumonia, etc., all of which are genuine concerns for me. The fact that this friend shares my deep faith in God, knowing that my days and hours are held in God's hand, is reassuring to me, too. I don't want to deceive myself about the reality of my health issues, but it's up to God as to how many days, weeks, months, etc. are still ahead of me.

My health challenges include osteoporosis, scoliosis, some compression fractures, and a bulging disc I've had for many years. Over the years I've experienced an increasing amount of pain in my lower back due to a pinched nerve, but I won't allow that to keep me from doing as much as I can as often as I can.

A number of years ago I had an MRI (magnetic resonance image) taken. It was quite a challenge to get this inflexible body of mine into that tube-like machine. I and everyone helping me ended up doing many contortions to get the job done. But everyone involved was patient, kind, and understanding. They were open to my suggestions throughout the process. We were even able to laugh a few times as we struggled. It was interesting that, before the MRI, my wheelchair was about 10 feet away and someone asked if I was able to walk to the MRI machine. No!

It's been several years since I had to give up driving my tractors or doing any kind of farm work. I'll never stop missing going out to the field. Giving up driving a vehicle has also been difficult. It was just too hard for Rita to transfer me from my wheelchair to the seat of our van.

Rita is such an amazing person. In all the time she's cared for me, I've never had pressure sores or any kind of skin breakdown, which many people in my situation go through. Cleanliness and proper nutrition have been an important part of both our lives, and she has done a marvelous job of managing this throughout the years.

Again, all those things are in God's hands.

I've expressed to many people that, while I don't have a death wish, I definitely have a "heaven wish." While I've seen God's blessing at every turn in my life, I can't begin to describe the excitement I feel at knowing that when I pass from this world to the next, I'll leave my wheelchair behind. I will finally know what it's like to walk, dance, even run! Things I can barely imagine doing since I never had that ability.

When I get to heaven, I want to jump into Jesus' lap, get a big hug, then run a triple marathon. As a Christian I know that, as 2 Corinthians 5:8 says, "to be absent from the body is to be present with the Lord." According to John 14:6, which says, "I am the way the truth and the life, no one comes to the Father except through me," my faith that Jesus paid the debt for my sins is what qualifies me to spend eternity with God. For me, the idea that I'll be freed from this confining earthly body at the moment of death, is something I look forward to with anticipation and not dread.

There's never been a time in my life when I felt like God had shortchanged me. I credit my parents for setting the stage for me to know that I could reach my dreams. I needed some help and I've had to do some things differently than others, but I'm thankful that I was able to live the life I dreamed of.

My good friend, Roy Peters, once told me, "Harlan, your cerebral palsy wasn't any accident and didn't happen by chance. God can use your situation. You can be an inspiration and encouragement to everyone in your life." As I advance in age, I certainly see what he meant.

Every person's life is a gift, and when we have Christ in our lives, that gift becomes even more valuable. I was 18 when I invited Jesus to be part of my life at a revival meeting. As I've said over and over, my parents had great faith in God, so that was nothing new to me. What was missing though was my own personal commitment to living in the same godly manner that I experienced in my family.

At that age, I could have taken a rebellious, angry road. From many people's perspective, it may have looked like I only had misery and pain waiting for me along life's way. But look what God did along the way! He has used every part of my life to teach me and give me opportunities to bless others.

As I've undergone therapy all these years, I can clearly see that, no matter who you're helping, it's beneficial to give them lots of encouragement and help them recognize the reward of persistence. Not all my ventures went smoothly – at least at first. We're all human, we make mistakes. If we can learn from them and keep going, that's a reward in itself.

Over the years I've been teased about spending too much time talking to people. But through my insurance business, through working with different therapists, and just interacting with people in general I have learned that it's so important to take time to really know people and invest in their lives.

While you're at it, don't forget to add some humor to the task. Laughter is so good for our soul. It helps break barriers down and lessens tense situations. Just the sight of a warm, friendly smile can help others relax. In almost every situation a friendly smile can have a positive effect.

Of course, most of us have a dream or two that seem unlikely to happen, maybe even unrealistic. But we should never rob one of their dreams. I have experienced the benefit of helping people – and myself – to overcome our toughest obstacles. Miracles do happen. Maybe a dream requires gentle redirection. Whatever the case, dare to dream and follow the road to make dreams a reality.

My parents never mentioned the difficulties they experienced in caring for me or my sister Joanie, who was born with Down Syndrome. They didn't focus on themselves or the battles it would take to accomplish what was necessary. They didn't allow us to focus on ourselves, either. We thought about others, what they needed and how we could help. We learned that every connection we have with others is important and we need to view those connections that way.

If you encounter or know someone like me, it's so helpful to get down to their eye level. That gives them a sense of equality, a greater personal connection, and you're less intimidating than if you stand over them.

All my life, just an inch or two on the mechanical modifications I used, the height to get into or out of a building or vehicle, reach at table, etc. has been critical. It could mean the difference between success or frustration.

When we deal with others, that inch or two is equally important. There's an old saying about going the extra mile. Be aware that sometimes all we need to do is push through one extra inch. We should be willing to do it.

One of the most important things we can do in life is have a passion for living. Respecting and listening to those around us will give us wisdom and insight we won't find anywhere else.

Whatever we do, working as a team greatly strengthens our efforts and helps pool our knowledge. No matter what our capabilities, each of us holds in our hands the ability to make a difference in someone else's life. Every day we should give our best. You can be sure those efforts will bring blessings back to you.

I know from personal experience that having a genuine, caring heart that's focused on serving others takes us far, even further than we can imagine.

While I am deeply appreciative for all the blessings I've experienced throughout my life, death is not intimidating to me. For followers of Jesus, death means heaven, happiness, and Him. I don't have a death wish, but I do have a heaven wish. In the meantime, I'm going to live life to the fullest possible measure as God enables me.

Harlan and Rita Temple

Loretta Sorensen

I appreciate the work my editor, Loretta Sorensen, has done to help me tell my life story. Her writing career spans more than 30 years and she has assisted nearly 20 other authors like me in developing their books. Loretta and her husband Alan have two married daughters and three "awesome" grandchildren. The two of them have worked together since they married more than 50 years ago to raise and work Belgian draft horses on their small farm outside Yankton, South Dakota. Loretta says her first published article was about their beautiful horses. In the summer of 2021, the Sorensens treated Rita and me to a ride with one of their Belgian teams, Babe and Bob. That was a new and enjoyable experience for both me and Rita. Pictured below are Alan and Loretta in the driver's seat; Alan's cousin, Delano Christensen (standing) and his wife Marilyn Christensen; me, and sitting next to me, peeking around the wagon seat, is Rita.

"He is the one
we proclaim, admonishing
and teaching everyone
with all wisdom, so that we
may present everyone fully
mature in Christ. To this
end I strenuously contend
with all the energy Christ so
powerfully works in me."

COLOSSIANS 1:28